FOREWORD

This is my first book, and I have been lucky in that I had a publisher and topic to begin with, unlike a lot of writers who have it the other way round. It is said that there is a book in all of us; it just needs something to kick start it!

I love Enfield; I have lived here for most of my life. That was why I felt proud and honoured when I was asked to write this book. This history is by no means comprehensive; I have given what are really the basic facts. I refer you to the bibliography so that you can explore further.

I must acknowledge the help of Graham Dalling, Librarian at the Enfield Local History Unit, for his guidance and opinions, especially when I went horribly wrong. He was extremely helpful and pulled no punches. Also, my thanks to his able assistant Kate Godfrey for her valuable work in sorting out the photographs I needed.

Stephen Hoye
Enfield 2005

DEDICATION

This book is dedicated to my wife Joan - thank you for your love and support.

ENFIELD
A HISTORY & CELEBRATION

STEPHEN G HOYE

THE FRANCIS FRITH COLLECTION

www.francisfrith.com

First published in the United Kingdom in 2005
by The Francis Frith Collection®

Hardback Edition 2005 ISBN 1-84589-200-3
Paperback Edition 2011 ISBN 978-1-84589-586-0

Text and Design copyright © The Francis Frith Collection®
Photographs copyright © The Francis Frith Collection®
except where indicated

The Frith® photographs and the Frith® logo are reproduced under licence from Heritage Photographic Resources Ltd, the owners of the Frith® archive and trademarks
'The Francis Frith Collection', 'Francis Frith' and 'Frith' are registered trademarks of Heritage Photographic Resources Ltd.

All rights reserved. No photograph in this publication may be sold to a third party other than in the original form of this publication, or framed for sale to a third party. No parts of this publication may be reproduced, stored in a retrieval system, or transmitted, in any form, or by any means, electronic, mechanical, photocopying, recording or otherwise, without the prior permission of the publishers and copyright holder.

British Library Cataloguing in Publication Data

Enfield - A History & Celebration
Stephen G Hoye

The Francis Frith Collection
Oakley Business Park, Wylye Road,
Dinton, Wiltshire SP3 5EU
Tel: +44 (0) 1722 716 376
Email: info@francisfrith.co.uk
www.francisfrith.com

Printed and bound in England

Front Cover: **ENFIELD, MARKET PLACE c1950** E179003t

Additional modern photographs by Stephen G Hoye, unless otherwise specified.

Domesday extract used in timeline by kind permission of
Alecto Historical Editions, www.domesdaybook.org
Aerial photographs reproduced under licence from
Simmons Aerofilms Limited.
Historical Ordnance Survey maps reproduced under licence from
Homecheck.co.uk

Every attempt has been made to contact copyright holders of illustrative material. We will be happy to give full acknowledgement in future editions for any items not credited. Any information should be directed to The Francis Frith Collection.

*The colour-tinting in this book is for illustrative purposes only,
and is not intended to be historically accurate*

AS WITH ANY HISTORICAL DATABASE, THE FRANCIS FRITH ARCHIVE IS CONSTANTLY BEING CORRECTED AND IMPROVED, AND THE PUBLISHERS WOULD WELCOME INFORMATION ON OMISSIONS OR INACCURACIES

CONTENTS

6   Timeline

8   Chapter One: From Little Acorns

28 Chapter Two: The Victorian Era

50 Chapter Three: Early Modernisation

82 Chapter Four: Modern Enfield

106 Chapter Five: Into the 21st Century

117 Acknowledgements and Bibliography

119 Free Mounted Print Offer

ENFIELD FROM THE AIR 1920 AF1542

ENFIELD
A HISTORY & CELEBRATION

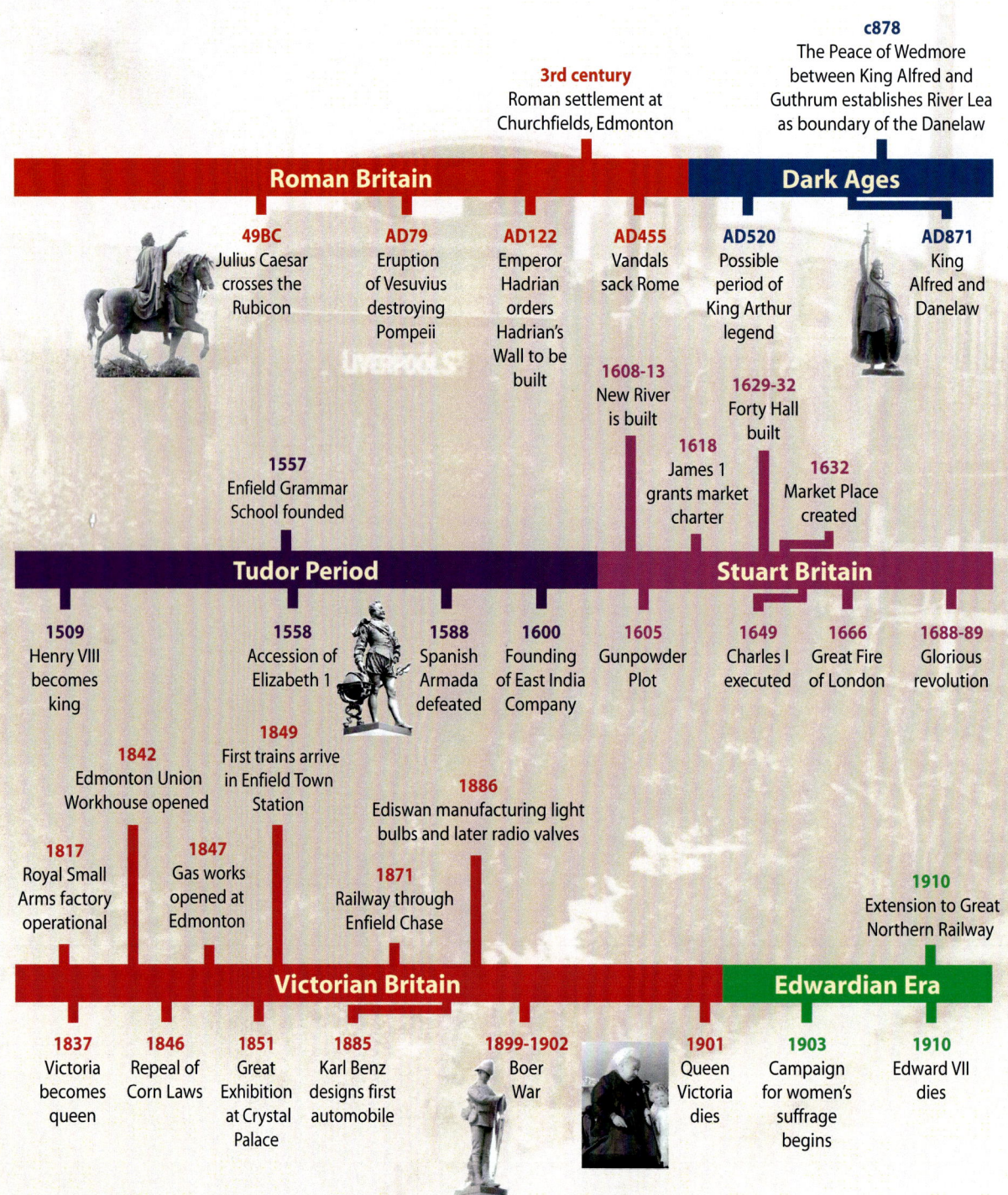

Roman Britain

- **3rd century** — Roman settlement at Churchfields, Edmonton
- **49BC** — Julius Caesar crosses the Rubicon
- **AD79** — Eruption of Vesuvius destroying Pompeii
- **AD122** — Emperor Hadrian orders Hadrian's Wall to be built
- **AD455** — Vandals sack Rome

Dark Ages

- **c878** — The Peace of Wedmore between King Alfred and Guthrum establishes River Lea as boundary of the Danelaw
- **AD520** — Possible period of King Arthur legend
- **AD871** — King Alfred and Danelaw

Tudor Period

- **1557** — Enfield Grammar School founded
- **1509** — Henry VIII becomes king
- **1558** — Accession of Elizabeth 1
- **1588** — Spanish Armada defeated
- **1600** — Founding of East India Company

Stuart Britain

- **1608-13** — New River is built
- **1618** — James 1 grants market charter
- **1629-32** — Forty Hall built
- **1632** — Market Place created
- **1605** — Gunpowder Plot
- **1649** — Charles I executed
- **1666** — Great Fire of London
- **1688-89** — Glorious revolution

Victorian Britain

- **1842** — Edmonton Union Workhouse opened
- **1849** — First trains arrive in Enfield Town Station
- **1886** — Ediswan manufacturing light bulbs and later radio valves
- **1817** — Royal Small Arms factory operational
- **1847** — Gas works opened at Edmonton
- **1871** — Railway through Enfield Chase
- **1837** — Victoria becomes queen
- **1846** — Repeal of Corn Laws
- **1851** — Great Exhibition at Crystal Palace
- **1885** — Karl Benz designs first automobile
- **1899-1902** — Boer War
- **1901** — Queen Victoria dies

Edwardian Era

- **1910** — Extension to Great Northern Railway
- **1903** — Campaign for women's suffrage begins
- **1910** — Edward VII dies

HISTORICAL TIMELINE FOR ENFIELD

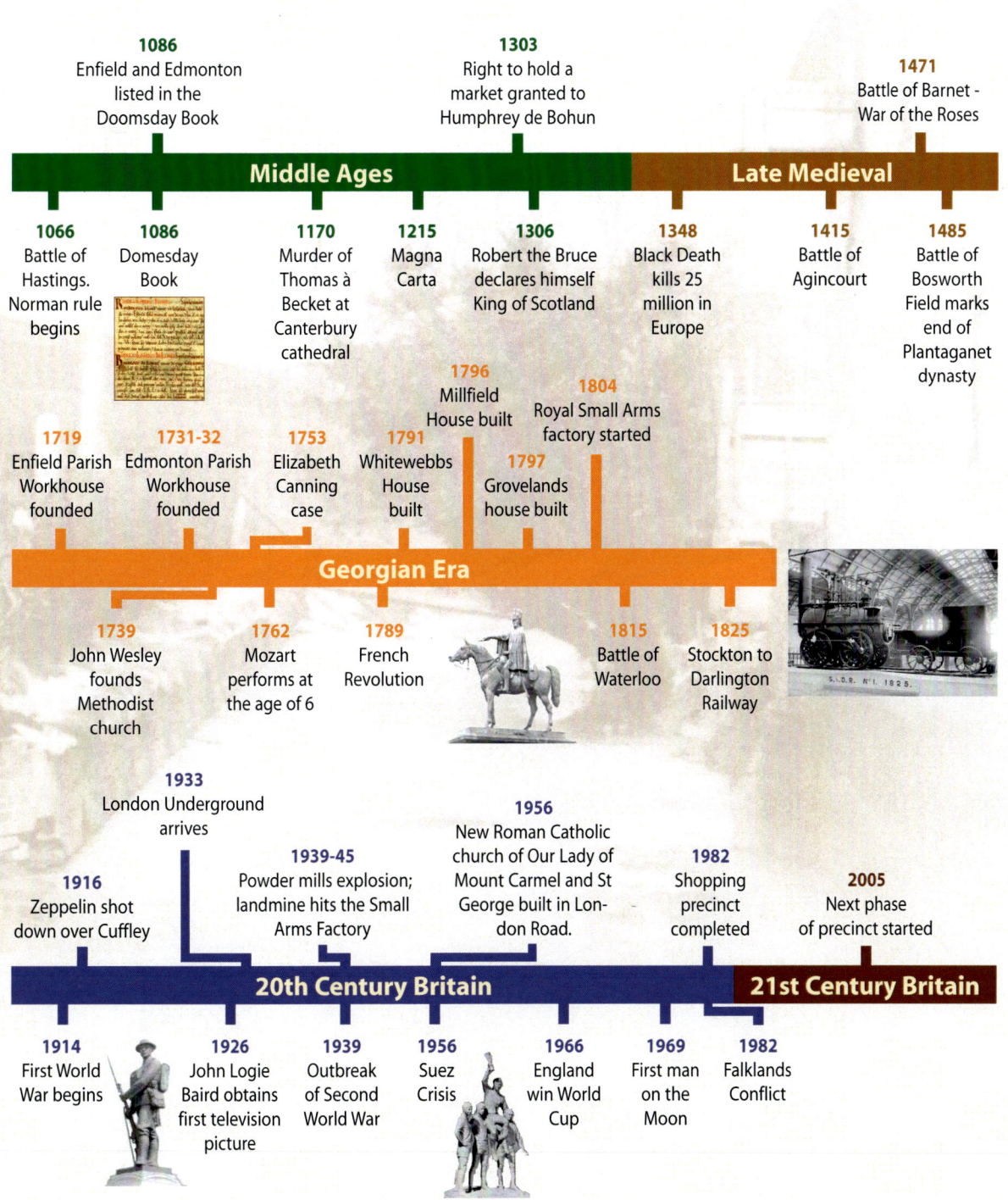

Middle Ages | Late Medieval

1086 – Enfield and Edmonton listed in the Doomsday Book
1303 – Right to hold a market granted to Humphrey de Bohun
1471 – Battle of Barnet - War of the Roses

1066 – Battle of Hastings. Norman rule begins
1086 – Domesday Book
1170 – Murder of Thomas à Becket at Canterbury cathedral
1215 – Magna Carta
1306 – Robert the Bruce declares himself King of Scotland
1348 – Black Death kills 25 million in Europe
1415 – Battle of Agincourt
1485 – Battle of Bosworth Field marks end of Plantaganet dynasty

Georgian Era

1719 – Enfield Parish Workhouse founded
1731-32 – Edmonton Parish Workhouse founded
1753 – Elizabeth Canning case
1791 – Whitewebbs House built
1796 – Millfield House built
1797 – Grovelands house built
1804 – Royal Small Arms factory started

1739 – John Wesley founds Methodist church
1762 – Mozart performs at the age of 6
1789 – French Revolution
1815 – Battle of Waterloo
1825 – Stockton to Darlington Railway

20th Century Britain | 21st Century Britain

1916 – Zeppelin shot down over Cuffley
1933 – London Underground arrives
1939-45 – Powder mills explosion; landmine hits the Small Arms Factory
1956 – New Roman Catholic church of Our Lady of Mount Carmel and St George built in London Road.
1982 – Shopping precinct completed
2005 – Next phase of precinct started

1914 – First World War begins
1926 – John Logie Baird obtains first television picture
1939 – Outbreak of Second World War
1956 – Suez Crisis
1966 – England win World Cup
1969 – First man on the Moon
1982 – Falklands Conflict

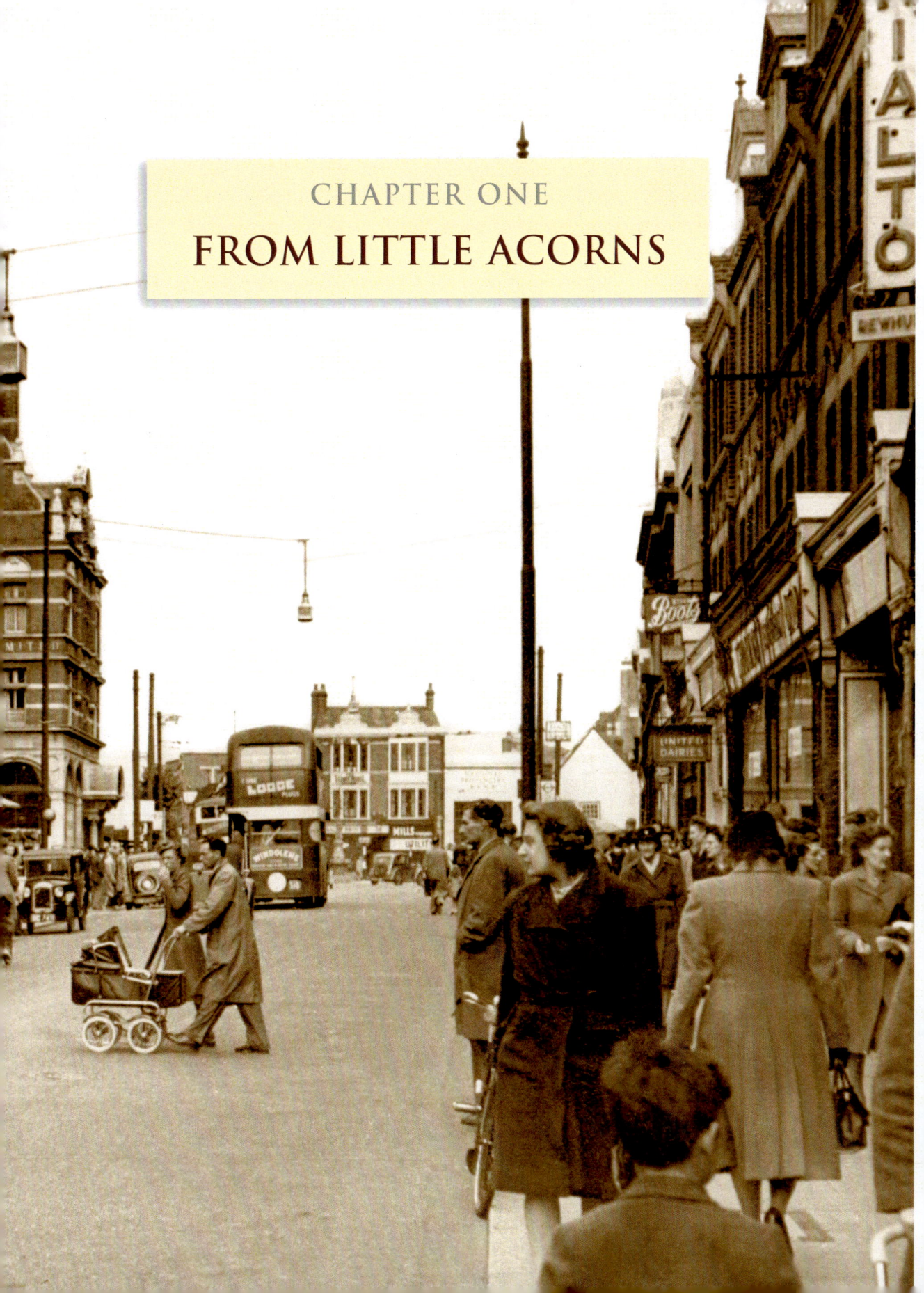

CHAPTER ONE
FROM LITTLE ACORNS

A HISTORY & CELEBRATION

LIKE most of our towns and cities, Enfield has had humble beginnings. Now the northernmost borough in the Greater London area, it has seen amazing changes, from being a small rural community, then an industrialised borough, and now a commercial centre. There are still bits and pieces left to tell us of Enfield's past but, as in other places, these are dwindling as the years pass. Enfieldians are proud of their heritage, and proud of what has been achieved within the borough. The borough is not just Enfield Town, but also includes Edmonton and Southgate - Southgate did not become an individual area until 1881.

FORTY HILL, MAIDENS BRIDGE c1955 F186012

Enfield's history begins with the Roman invasion. Unfortunately, not much of the Roman period actually survives. There were several settlements along Ermine Street up to the early 5th century. At Churchfields, Edmonton, the remains of a 3rd-century settlement was found. The only other remains we know of were excavated at Bush Hill Park between 1974 and 1976 when the land was being cleared for redevelopment. When the Romans finally left British shores, most of what they had achieved fell into disrepair.

The Saxon hordes that took their place brought with them their own culture and living standards. A small settlement was made in Enfield - the name is derived from Anglo-Saxon, and means 'field belonging to Eana'. During the reign of King Offa, in about 790, Edmonton was given to St Albans Abbey. In the ninth century Alfred was King of Wessex, the dominant Anglo-Saxon kingdom at that time. Other parts of England had been overrun by the Danes, and the armies of Wessex and the Danes had been warring with each other for a decade. The Danes had the upper hand for a long time, but they were eventually beaten at the battle of Edington in 878. A treaty was drawn up between Alfred and the Danish king Guthrum, with the boundary between their territories formed by the River Lea. Enfield was therefore on the eastern edge of the Saxon kingdoms of Wessex and Mercia, while on the other side of the River Lea was King Guthrum and the Danelaw. In 894 the Danes did sail 20 miles up the Lea, but the river's marshy banks were a hindrance to their travelling out of their territory. The marsh at Edmonton was approximately half-a-mile wide, and was criss-crossed by other watercourses.

By 1066 the manors of Enfield and Edmonton were ruled over by Ansgar the Staller. By the year 1086, the year when William the Conqueror ordered the Domesday Book to be compiled, the two manors were in the hands of Geoffrey de Mandeville, and they remained with the de Mandeville family until 1189. The manor of Enfield then passed through various families before coming to the

FROM LITTLE ACORNS

CHURCH STREET c1945 E179002

At just before or after the end of the Second World War, Enfield is looking lively again. Note the position of the street lamps.

de Bohun family, who inherited it in 1266. In 1303, Edward I granted Humphrey de Bohun the right to hold a weekly market in Enfield and also two or three week-long fairs. (In 2003, Queen Elizabeth visited Enfield with Prince Philip and presented the Old Enfield Charitable Trust, who run the market, with a plaque to celebrate its 700th anniversary.)

The de Bohun family held Enfield manor until 1419. It was then held by Henry V, whose father had married one of the de Bohun daughters, and the king granted the manor to Queen Catherine in 1422. The manor remained in the Duchy of Lancaster (it was granted in dower to Margaret of Anjou and then Elizabeth Woodville, wife of Edward IV) until 1550, when Edward VI granted it for life to his sister Princess Elizabeth.

The manor of Edmonton was held by the de Say family. They had inherited it through a split in the de Mandeville estate in 1284. The de Says controlled the manor of Edmonton until 1361, when it passed to Adam Francis, a mercer. The manor was then divided again until 1461, when it was reunited under Sir Thomas Charlton. Sir Thomas was succeeded by his son Sir Richard Charlton, a supporter of Richard III. He was killed at the Battle of Bosworth, and the manor and its lands were forfeited to the Crown.

In 1290 Edward I ('Longshanks') passed through Enfield. He was bringing the body of his beloved wife Eleanor of Castile back to London for burial. Just over the boundary he erected a cross where Waltham Cross is today; the cross marks the spot where the party stopped for the night.

The 15th century was dominated by the Wars of the Roses, a series of bloody battles for the crown of England between the Lancastrians on one side, and the Yorkists on the other. A part of Enfield saw action in

ENFIELD
A HISTORY & CELEBRATION

MARKET PLACE c1950 E179003t

Here we see a busy Saturday market. Note the be-ribboned car - it looks as if a bride has been safely delivered. The grand façade of Burton's rises behind.

ENFIELD

FROM LITTLE ACORNS

A HISTORY & CELEBRATION

1471, when the Battle of Barnet was fought on Enfield Chase.

Figures for losses in the battle are unreliable; it is said that 500 Yorkists and 1,000 Lancastrians were killed. The Battle of Barnet marked the demise of the most powerful baron of his time, Richard Neville, Warwick the Kingmaker - he was killed in the conflict, which is commemorated by an obelisk in the field where the battle was supposed to have taken place.

In 1557 Enfield Grammar School was founded. The school originated before the Reformation as a chantry foundation at St Andrew's Church. The school endures to this day, and is very popular with both pupils and parents. The building in Church Walk where the school is situated is dated around 1590.

In 1571 an Act of Parliament for improving navigation between London and Ware was passed. The River Lea was scoured and embanked in certain areas. By 1577 a pound lock (one of the earliest in the country) had been built at Waltham Abbey.

By 1572 the layout of the streets was more or less what it is today. The settlement was known then as Enfield Green. Coming from Barnet, a traveller would have come across Dolmans Bridge and reached a gate, which was level with Gentlemans Row/Church Street. Past the gate there were three cottages on the right (see the map, ZZZ05532, page 16). The map shows Parsonage Street, which is now called Silver Street, and Bury Lane, which is now Southbury Road. In 1572 other parts of Enfield were known by different names. Enfield Highway was known as Cocksmiths End, and Enfield Wash as Horsepoolstones.

WINCHMORE HILL, GROVELANDS PARK c1955 W482007

The lake is used for boating and fishing.

FROM LITTLE ACORNS

Fact File

QUEEN ELIZABETH II IN ENFIELD 2003 ZZZ05531 (Reproduced by courtesy of Peter Dyer)

Queen Elizabeth II is seen here on her walkabout around the market with Mrs Pam Taylor, the Chair of the Old Enfield Charitable Trust.

Enfield's market was instituted in 1303 by Edward I. This was a weekly market with two or three fairs a year (the written sources vary). In 2003 Queen Elizabeth and Prince Philip visited Enfield to present a plaque to commemorate the 700th anniversary of the market.

THE ENFIELD MARKET PLAQUE 2005
ZZZ05530 Stephen G Hoye

This is the plaque presented to Enfield by the Queen in 2003.

ENFIELD
A HISTORY & CELEBRATION

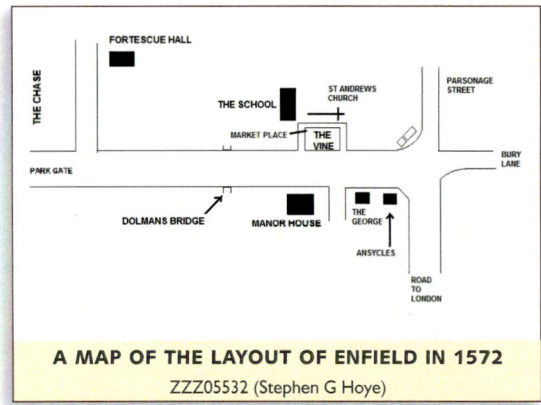

A MAP OF THE LAYOUT OF ENFIELD IN 1572
ZZZ05532 (Stephen G Hoye)

This shows the layout of Enfield town in 1572.

The manor house (known by locals as 'The Palace') was an E-shaped building facing north. The ground floor comprised a hall, a parlour, a buttery and a kitchen. Upstairs were many chambers, all magnificently furnished. The house belonged to the Crown, but was always leased to tenants. Through much of the Tudor period the Taylor family lived there, but in 1582 John Taylor found himself in debt, and he had to sell the lease to Henry Middlemore. The price

AN ENGRAVING OF ENFIELD MANOR HOUSE c1778
ZZZ05533 (Enfield Libraries Local History Unit)

Here we see an engraving of Enfield manor house, or 'Palace'. Although this dates from c1778, the original E shape of the building is clear to see.

was £1,318. Today, where the manor once stood is the site of Pearsons Ltd, the department store. Nothing remains of the original building.

HILLYFIELDS c1955 E179015

This peaceful scene, taken on a warm sunny day, shows Hillyfields, off Clay Hill.

CLAY HILL, THE ROSE AND CROWN c1955
E179016

The Rose and Crown is one of Clay Hill's two pubs. Note the absence of traffic.

By 1572 there were several settlements established around a part of Enfield known as Forty Green (now Forty Hill). There were cottages in Bulls Cross Lane (now Bulls Cross), and there were two small settlements in Whitewebbs Lane-Romey Street (at the Bulls Cross End) and Whitewebbs proper (near the King and Tinker). In Clay Hill lay the settlement of Bridge Street (near where the Rose and Crown now stands).

FROM LITTLE ACORNS

The focal point of Forty Hill in the 16th century was the great house of Elsynge, which lay between the site of Forty Hall and the Turkey Brook. The house belonged to Sir Thomas Lovell, Chancellor of the Exchequer to Henry VII. It became a royal palace in 1539 when Henry VIII persuaded its then owner, the Earl of Rutland, to swap the house for other properties. It was here in 1547 that Edward VI was told of the death of his father (Henry VIII) and of his own accession to the throne. Elizabeth I came to the throne in 1558. Her stays in Enfield were in 1564, 1568, 1572 and 1587. The first three occasions were at Elsynge Palace, and the fourth, in 1587, was at the manor house. It is here that the story of Sir Walter Raleigh and the laying of the cape for the queen to walk on is supposed to have taken place, but the story is highly questionable.

WHITEWEBBS PARK, THE POND c1955 E179020

The lake is used for fishing. This photograph was probably taken at the weekend - there are plenty of people about.

ENFIELD
A HISTORY & CELEBRATION

Enfield's war memorial stands on the corner of Chase Green.

CHASE SIDE c1950 E179005

In 1581 there were attempts to sabotage the River Lea. The banks were cut near Green Street, and there was an attempt to burn the lock at Waltham. The unrest was led by Enfield maltmen, who had lost business because malt and barley was being carried by river instead of by road. This was one of the main businesses that Enfield had a claim to in those early years.

At about the same period, a problem developed over Enfield Chase. Enfield Chase was an open area used by the nobility for hunting. In 1581 there was a clash over the enclosure of certain areas. Parts of the Chase were enclosed, various arguments ensued, and the enclosures were removed. This was not the last time this thorny subject was to come up, however.

The passing of Elizabeth I brought James I to the throne, the first of the Stuart dynasty. In 1606 the New River Company was set up by Act of Parliament to bring fresh water from springs near Ware to London. Construction began c1608-09 and was completed by 1613. The course of the New River has been considerably altered today, especially by the abandonment of the loops at Whitewebbs and New Southgate. The New River loop has been cleaned up, and work has been done on some the banks. There are also markers on the pavement showing its course. This work was done

FROM LITTLE ACORNS

themselves. One of these noblemen engaged the tinker in conversation, asking him what he thought of the current monarch. The tinker gave his views, which were not very complimentary. One of the party came up to the tinker, and whispered that he was talking to King James I himself. The tinker blushed, fell on his knees and begged forgiveness. It is said that the king asked for a sword and knighted him. Like many stories, this is probably more myth than truth.

AN ENGRAVING OF THEOBALDS PALACE
ZZZ05534 (Enfield Libraries Local History Unit)

Theobald's Palace was a favourite residence of James I. The remains of Theobald Palace are in Cedar Park, Theobald's Lane, in Waltham Cross.

by Thames Water and Enfield Preservation Society.

In 1618 James granted Enfield a market charter. The market that now operates on Thursday, Friday and Saturday can trace its origins to this charter. This period also saw the founding of another of Enfield's famous schools, Latymer, founded in 1624, which now stands in Haselbury Road. The current building dates from 1910.

There is a story concerning one of the public houses in the Crews Hill area, the King and Tinker. The story goes that one day a tinker was sitting drinking his ale. A group of noblemen, who had been hunting on Enfield Chase, rode up and ordered drinks for

In 1629 Sir Nicholas Rainton began building Forty Hall. Some of the brickwork used here was from the ruined Elsynge Palace. Rainton was a rich merchant - he had made his money by importing satin and taffeta from Florence. An active businessman, Rainton remained in the city long after he moved to Forty Hall. He was a leading member of the Haberdashers' Company, became an Alderman of the City of London in 1621, Sheriff in 1621-22, and Lord Mayor in 1632 before being knighted. Forty Hall was completed in 1636. Rainton was imprisoned in 1640 after he refused to lend money to Charles I and failed to supply details of the wealth of his associates when requested to do so by the Crown. He was taken to the Marshalsea before being moved to the Tower with four other aldermen, but after public demonstrations they were released after five days. His public activities ceased after the outbreak of the Civil War in 1642, and he retired to Forty Hall. By the time of his death his son, daughter-in-law, and all six children were dead, together with his wife Lady Rebecca.

> ### Fact File
>
> *Enfield and Edmonton are listed in the Domesday Book under Edmonton Hundred. The Domesday Book was ordered to be compiled by William I (the Conqueror) in 1086. Property and its ownership were listed so that the king could gain maximum profit from taxes.*

The Great Plague which hit London in 1664-65 was the origin of another apocryphal story of Enfield. It is said that the green which bounds Windmill Hill and Chase Green was used as a burial site for victims of the plague. The story goes on to say that if the area were to be dug up, the plague would be unleashed again. It is not known if there is any truth in this.

The workhouse system that prevailed nationally during the 18th and 19th centuries became established early in the 18th century in both Enfield and Edmonton parishes. Enfield's workhouse was founded in 1719, but it was another thirteen or fourteen years before Edmonton had its workhouse, which was originally in Church Street. When it moved, what remained formed the basis of what is now North Middlesex Hospital.

In 1753 the strange case of Elizabeth Canning came to light. She was a maidservant, and claimed that she had been abducted and been forced to become a prostitute; however, she ended up being convicted for perjury. It seems that she reappeared at her mother's house after being missing for a month. She claimed that she had been kidnapped, and that during the month she had been missing she had been forced into a carriage and taken to a brothel in Enfield. Here the madam, Susannah Wells, had tried to force her to become a prostitute. She said that she had refused, whereupon Mary Squires had cut off her stays and she was locked up. During this time she was fed only bread and water. At last she managed to break out and get home.

After telling her story, Canning was taken to Enfield by a posse. There Wells and Squires were arrested and taken before the magistrate (the novelist Henry Fielding), who also took Canning's deposition on February 7. He interrogated a girl named Virtue Hall, a prostitute from Wells's brothel. At first Hall claimed that she had never seen Canning, let

FROM LITTLE ACORNS

THE TOWN CENTRE c1950 E179012

This shows how Enfield used to be, not the noisy hubbub that there is today. Could the photograph have been taken on a Sunday?

alone witnessing Squires robbing her, but Fielding forced her to support Canning's story lest she be sentenced as a felon. The trial against Squires and Wells began at the Old Bailey a month later. Squires said that she had been in Dorset at the time Canning had claimed she had robbed her, and a local priest could prove it. Wells was sentenced to branding on the thumb. Squires was sentenced to be hanged for stealing Canning's stays. John Gibson, William Clark, and Thomas Grevil, who had testified that they had seen Squires in Dorset, were to be tried for perjury. However, the chief magistrate, the Lord Mayor of London, was dissatisfied with the verdict. He appealed to George II, and the king granted first a stay in execution and eventually a pardon. In May 1754 Canning was indicted for perjury and jailed in Newgate prison.

The three men who had testified for Squires were also pardoned when no one appeared to testify against them. Many people, several contemporary luminaries among them, tried to have their say in the matter. Some vandals broke the windows of the mayor's coach and mockingly called him 'the King of Gypsies'. Soon people all over Britain had divided to two factions: 'Canaanites', who supported Canning, and 'Egyptians', who supported Mary Squires. Those who disbelieved Canning suggested that she might have been in hiding because of an illegitimate pregnancy or an abortion. Both sides published a number of pamphlets in which they criticized and ridiculed the other side. Fielding wrote one to defend Canning and himself when his opponent Dr John Hill mocked him and defended Squires. Canning was found guilty of perjury, and was sentenced to penal transportation to the American colonies for seven years and forbidden to return during that time on pain of death. Some of her influential supporters in the East India Company arranged her trip so that she was taken to America in comfort instead of in a convict ship. She sailed for America on 31 July 1754. Elizabeth Cooke, wife of a governor of the Bank of England, arranged a £100 trust that was to be paid to Canning when she returned. Canning kept quiet about the case in her later life. In America, she moved to Wethersfield, Connecticut and lodged with a minister, Elisha Williams. She married John Treat, a great-nephew of the Governor of Connecticut, and had five children. She died in 1773 at the age of 38.

In the late 18th century and early 19th century some important houses were built. These were Whitewebbs House, built in 1791 for Dr Abraham Wilkinson; Capel House, built in 1793 for a former governor of Bombay; Millfield House, Edmonton, 1796; Grovelands House, built in 1797, designed by John Nash with gardens laid out by Humphrey Repton; and Myddleton House, built in 1818 for Henry Carington Bowles. All of these are still standing today. Whitewebbs House is now a restaurant, Capel House is part of the Capel Manor Horticultural Centre, Millfield House has been converted and is now the Millfield Theatre, and Grovelands House is now a private hospital. Myddleton House now belongs to the Lee Valley Regional Park Authority, and the surrounding area is used for camping and caravanning.

WHITEWEBBS HOUSE c1955 E179017

FROM LITTLE ACORNS

SOUTHGATE, GROVELANDS HOSPITAL c1955 S641046

This grandeur is not what one usually associates with hospital treatment.

Although there had been some kinds of industry in Enfield in medieval times, for instance the flour mill, Enfield's first real factory did not start its working life until 1816. This was the Royal Small Arms Factory. Its birth was due to the unsatisfactory situation of the previous 100 years, when the governments of the day were mostly supplied with arms from Birmingham, Liege and Hamburg, but these were not of a good enough standard. An ordnance factory was set up in Lewisham, but this too was unsatisfactory. By 1811 the manufacture of ordnance had moved to the powder mill at Waltham Abbey. Here, water from the River Lea was used to power the mill. Major Mulcaster, who had completed a survey of the building, said that the water of the Lea was sufficient for the powder mill, but a factory to make other ordnance should, he suggested, be at a site just south of this.

Fact File

The novelist Henry Fielding (author of 'Tom Jones') had connections with Enfield. He was the magistrate involved in the strange case of Elizabeth Canning, who alleged that she had been abducted. She was afterwards convicted of perjury, and was transported to America.

A HISTORY & CELEBRATION

In April 1816 John Rennie made an eligibility study of the site. His view was that there was sufficient water, and that as barges were serving the powder mill, these could also serve the factory. There were some difficulties to be overcome over rights and tenancies, but in 1817 the whole operation was switched from Lewisham to the new factory at Enfield Lock. So began a long relationship between the Small Arms Factory and Enfield - the factory eventually closed in 1988. There is a museum on the site, but the rest has been redeveloped and is now Enfield Garden Village. The story of the Royal Small Arms Factory is a history in itself. There are many books on the subject: the best is 'The Royal Small Arms Factory, Enfield and Its Workers' by David Pam, published by the author.

> **Fact File**
>
> *The rifle that became the main infantry weapon through three wars was developed and made in Enfield. This was the Lee Enfield rifle. Although no longer used by the British Army, it is still used in some parts of the Commonwealth.*

It is incredible to think that even back in the late 18th and early 19th centuries public transport was beginning to play a part in the life of the borough. Before the arrival of the railways, passenger traffic to and from Enfield and Edmonton was largely in the hands of the stagecoach. (From the 1830s onwards,

THE ROYAL SMALL ARMS FACTORY ZZZ05535 (Enfield Libraries Local History Unit)

Here we see part of the works of RSAF. The water area was eventually filled in.

FROM LITTLE ACORNS

these vehicles were progressively replaced by the larger-bodied horse omnibuses.) Enfield was also served by long-distance stagecoaches travelling along the Hertford Road. In 1826 coaches passed through Enfield on their way from London to Boston, Cambridge, Edinburgh, Fakenham, Kings Lynn, Stamford, Wisbech and York. By travelling via Enfield, Royston and Huntingdon, it was possible to avoid Highgate Hill and Barnet Hill on the Great North Road.

In 1790 Thomas Kimpton's coaches were making six return journeys daily between the Golden Lion at Edmonton Green and the Bull Inn, Bishopsgate. His rival James Dickenson was making five return journeys daily between Enfield and London, calling at the Bull Inn, Bishopsgate and the Castle and Falcon, Aldersgate.

By 1825 there were seventeen coaches operating between London and Edmonton which made 39 return journeys daily. Five coaches were operating between London and Ponders End, making three return journeys daily. Just one vehicle was operating between London and Southgate, managing one return journey daily. By 1839 there were four operators between Edmonton and Bishopsgate. Mr J Willis was operating two omnibuses and one stagecoach. Messrs S and J Isaac had three omnibuses and two coaches. Joseph St John had three omnibuses and one coach. William Matthews junior had just one coach.

This brings us nicely on to a ghostly tale involving the London to Cambridge stagecoach. In eastern Enfield there is a local park called Albany Park. It has been reported in the local press that residents in the area have seen this stagecoach, which appears on Christmas Eve heading north to Cambridge. It travels about three feet off the ground, showing where the road was then; it only seems to appear when it is a moonlight night. The author must stress that he has never seen it, but he did meet residents who have.

The enclosure of the Enfield Chase saw the creation of two new estates. Francis Russell, the surveyor responsible for the enclosure, acquired 152 acres of land on which he built himself a mansion: Beech Hill Park. Elsewhere on the Chase, Richard Jebb, a popular society doctor, was granted a lease on three adjoining plots of former Chase land. He built a house which he named Trent Place. It was named after Trento in the Tyrol, where in 1777 Jebb had cured the Duke of Gloucester, brother of King George III, of a serious illness. This house was progressively enlarged by successive owners and came to be known as Trent Park.

Fact File

Enfield Grammar School occupies a building known as Enfield Court, which stands on the corner of Baker Street and Parsonage Lane. This was formerly the home firstly of General John Martin, and then of Sir Alfred Somerset.

ENFIELD A HISTORY & CELEBRATION

FORTY HILL, THE GOAT c1955 F186002

SOUTHGATE, YE OLDE CHERRY TREE c1955 S641019

Although these are not actually coaching inns, it was these kind of establishments that the coaches used as calling points.

FROM LITTLE ACORNS

GENTLEMAN'S ROW c1965 E179045

Gentleman's Row faces Chase Green, where royalty came to hunt. Some of houses date back to Tudor times. The poet and author Charles Lamb once lived in Gentleman's Row.

CHAPTER TWO
THE VICTORIAN ERA

A HISTORY & CELEBRATION

PALMERS GREEN, BROOMFIELD PARK c1960 P295019

AT the start of the Victorian era, all the roads around Enfield had been turnpiked. These were under the care of the Commissioners for Turnpike Roads, who charged a uniform toll of 3d. This system lasted for another 30 years. In 1864 an Act was passed whereby from 1 July 1872 the turnpikes disappeared and the turnpike roads came under the care of the local boards of health. This applied to all parts of Enfield, whose Local Board of Health employed a local surveyor to ensure that the condition for funds was satisfied. The reason for this was that the money would come from the metropolitan counties.

Just before the enforcement of this Act, a connection was finally made to Chingford. Up to 1869 there had been no road link for seven miles west to east from Waltham Abbey to Water Lane. This put a burden on the merchants, as a hefty toll was levied. Some public-spirited people raised firstly £500, then £700, to build an extension to the road which had ended at the River Lea; the new extension took it into Chingford. This road is still in use today - it is now known as the Lea Valley Road.

It would be another twelve years before the road system saw any further changes. Up to 1881, public road transport was provided by local coaching firms and the national stagecoach network. A company known as the North London Suburban Tram Company eventually, after some difficulty, ran a service operated by horse-drawn trams; but after some poor results, which it blamed on the weather, the company went into receivership. (They had wanted to use steam trams, but were not allowed to do so, because the steam trams caused a spate of broken rails.) They were eventually taken over by the North Metropolitan Tramways Company in 1901.

Although the time table shown below is that of the Eastern Counties' Railway Company, it was the Northern & Eastern Railway Company who in 1840 pushed the railway through Enfield and built the line from Stratford to Broxbourne. There were stations at Water Lane (now Angel Road), at Ponders End, and eventually at the Ordnance Factory (now Enfield Lock) in 1855.

By 1844 the railway company operating the line had changed: the Northern & Eastern Railway Company were unprofitable, and the line was now in the hands of the Eastern Counties' Railway Company. They realised that a branch to Enfield Town would be a good source of revenue. Each railway line needed an Act of Parliament; a bill was laid before Parliament in 1846 and was duly passed. The branch line left the main line just after Water Lane and headed in a north-westerly direction.

EASTERN COUNTIES' RAILWAY TIME TABLE.

DOWN TRAINS.

WEEK DAYS.	Parl	1&2	Parl	Parl.	1&2	1 2 3	1 2 3	1 2 3	1&2	1 2 3	1 2 3	1&2	1&2	1&2	1 2 3	1 2 3	1 2 3	1 2 3	1 2 3	1 2 3	1&2	1 2 3	1 2 3
LEAVE	a.m.	a.m.	a.m.	a.m.	a.m.	a.m.	p.m.	p.m.	p.m.	p.m.	p.m.	p.m.	p.m	p.m.	p.m.	p.m.	p.m	p.m.	p m.	p.m.	p.m.	p.m.	p.m.
LONDON	6 27	8 0	9 3	9 30	10 57	12 0	12 45	2 0	2 30	3 10	3 30	4 5	4 40	5 10	5 20	6 10	6 20	7 20	7 35	8 20	8 40	9 20	11 30
Mile End	6 35	...	9 6	...	...	12 3	...	...	...	3 13	...	...	...	...	...	...	...	...	...	...	...	...	...
Stratford ......[stow, &c.	6 45	...	9 16	9 41	...	12 13	...	2 12	2 41	3 23	...	...	4 50	5 20	5 30	6 22	...	7 30	...	8 30	...	9 31	11 40
Lea Bridge, *for Waltham-*	6 52	...	9 24	...	...	12 20	1 0	2 19	2 49	3 30	3 46	...	4 56	...	5 37	...	6 37	7 37	...	8 37	...	9 38	11 46
Tottenham	6 58	...	9 30	9 51	...	12 26	1 5	2 25	2 55	3 36	3 52	...	5 1	...	5 43	6 32	...	7 43	7 53	8 43	...	9 44	11 52
Park	7 2	...	9 35	...	...	12 31	...	2 30	3 0	3 41	3 56	...	...	...	5 47	...	6 44	7 47	...	8 47	...	9 47	11 56
Water Lane	7 7	...	9 40	9 56	...	12 35	...	2 34	...	3 45	4 0	...	...	...	5 52	6 37	6 48	7 52	7 59	8 52	...	9 53	12 1
Enfield } Edmonton	...	...	9 43	...	...	12 38	...	2 38	...	3 49	...	...	5 10	...	5 55	...	6 53	7 56	...	8 56	...	9 57	...
Branch } Enfield	...	...	9 50	...	...	12 45	...	2 45	...	3 55	...	...	5 15	...	6 0	...	7 0	8 2	...	9 5	...	10 5	...
Ponder's End	7 15	...	...	10 3	...	...	1 16	On Saturdays only.	3 10	...	4 6	...	...	5 35	...	6 45	...	...	8 6	...	9 4	...	12 9
Ordnance Factory	*	...	...	10 8	...	...	1 22		*	...	...	...	...	...	...	6 51	...	...	...	...	...	...	12 14
Waltham	7 27	8 29	...	10 13	11 30	...	1 27		3 19	...	4 16	4 32	...	5 44	...	6 55	...	...	8 14	...	9 14	...	12 19
Cheshunt	7 34	...	...	10 19	...	...	1 33		3 23	...	4 22	...	...	5 49	...	7 2	...	...	8 20	...	9 20	...	...
Broxbourne, *arrival*	7 44	8 37	...	10 25	11 40	...	1 39		3 33	...	4 30	4 43	...	5 56	...	7 10	...	...	8 26	...	9 27	...	12 30
for Hoddesdon *depart*	...	8 53	...	10 28	...	...	1 42		..	...		4 49	...	5 58	...	7 13	...	...	8 29	...	9 38	...	12 35
Rye House	...	8 58	...	10 33	...	...	1 47		...	...		...	...	...	...	7 18	...	...	8 34	...	...	...	...
St. Margaret's	...	9 3	...	!0 38	...	...	1 52		...	...		4 58	...	6 8	...	7 23	...	...	8 39	...	9 44	...	12 45
Ware	...	9 8	...	10 43	...	...	1 58		...	...		5 4	...	6 13	...	7 28	...	...	8 44	...	9 51	...	12 52
HERTFORD	...	9 15	...	10 50	...	...	2 5		...	...		5 10	...	6 20	...	7 35	...	...	8 50	...	10 0	...	1 0

UP TRAINS.

WEEK DAYS	1 2 3	1 2 3	Parl	1&2	1&2	1&2	1 2 3	1 2 3		1 2 3	1 2 5	1 2 3		1 2 3	1 2 3	1 2 3	1 2 3	1&2	1 2 3	1 2 3	1&2	1 2 3
LEAVE	a.m.	a.m.	a.m.	a.m.	a.m.	a.m.	a.m.	a.m.		p.m.	p.m.	p.m.		p.m.	p.m.	p.m.	p.m.	p.m.	p.m.	p.m.	p.m.	p.m.
HERTFORD	7 20	...	8 0	8 20	...	9 30	...	11 15		...	On Saturdays only.	2 25		...	...	...	5 45	...	...	...	...	8 25
Ware	7 25	...	8 5	8 25	...	9 35	...	11 21		...		2 31		...	...	...	5 50	...	...	...	...	8 30
St. Margaret's	7 30	...	8 11	8 30	...	9 40	...	11 27		...		2 37		...	...	...	5 55	...	...	...	...	8 35
Rye House	...	...	8 15	...	...	...	...	11 33		...		2 43		...	...	...	6 0	...	...	...	...	8 40
Broxbourn, *arrival*	7 38	...	8 20	8 38	...	9 46	...	11 38		...		2 49		...	...	...	6 5	...	...	...	...	8 46
for Hoddesdon *depart*	7 40	...	8 23	8 50	...	9 48	...	11 52	12 2	...		3 0	3 5	...	...	...	6 8	6 58	...	...	8 23	8 50
Cheshunt	7 47	...	8 29	8 57	...	...	...	...	12 8	...		☞	3 10	...	...	...	6 15	..	...	...	...	8 56
Waltham	7 53	...	8 34	9 3	...	9 58	...	12 2	12 15	...			3 18	...	...	...	6 20	7 9	...	...	8 33	9 2
Ordnance Factory	...	...	8 38	...	...	...	..	...	12 19	...		...	3 22	...	...	...	6 24	...	...	...	...	...
Ponder's End	8 0	...	8 45	9 10	...	10 5	...	...	12 25	...		...	3 28	...	...	...	6 31	...	...	...	...	9 11
Enfield } Enfield	...	8 3	...	...	9 15	‡	10 5	...	...	1 30	3 15	...	...	4 5	5 30	6 15	...	...	7 15	8 10	...	...
Branch } Edmonton	...	8 8	...	...	9 20		10 10	...	...	1 35	3 20	...	...	4 10	5 35	6 20	...	...	7 20	8 15	...	...
Water Lane	...	8 12	8 52	...	...	...	10 14	...	12 32	1 40	...	...	3 33	4 15	...	6 26	6 37	7 18	7 25	8 20	...	9 19
Park	...	8 15	8 56	...	...	...	10 18	...	12 36	1 44	3 27	...	...	4 19	...	6 30	...	...	7 28	8 24	...	9 23
Tottenham	8 10	...	9 0	...	9 26	...	10 22	...	12 41	1 49	3 32	...	3 38	4 23	5 43	...	6 43	...	7 33	8 28	...	9 28
Lea Bridge	. .	8 24	9 7	...	9 32	...	10 29	...	12 48	1 54	3 37	...	3 44	4 29	...	6 38	...	...	7 38	8 34	...	9 35
Stratford	8 22	8 32	9 16	9 28	9 38	10 23	10 38	12 28	12 57	2 2	3 44	3 28	3 52	4 37	5 53	6 45	6 54	7 36	7 45	8 43	8 58	9 45
Mile End	...	...	...	...	...	...	...	...	1 6	2 12	...	...	...	4 47	...	6 55	...	...	7 55	...	...	9 55
LONDON	8 35	8 45	9 30	9 40	9 50	10 35	10 50	12 45	1 10	2 15	3 55	3 40	4 5	4 50	6 5	7 0	7 5	7 50	8 0	8 53	9 10	10 0

* *Calls when required, notice having been given to the Guard at the preceding Station.* ‡ *Horses and private carriages not conveyed by this Train.* ☞ *First and Second Class only.*

Sunday Trains: Leave London for Enfield at 9.45, 10.30, 2.30, 8.0, and 10.15. Leave Enfield for London at 8.45, 11.0, 1.20, 6.30, and 9.0 Leave London for Ponder's End, Ordnance Factory, and Waltham at 6.45, 8.45, 10.30, 1.30, 3.0, 6.10, 8.40, 9.20. Waltham for London at 9.0, 11.5 11.55, 4.40, 7.29, and 9.2. Ordnance Factory at 9.5, 11.9, 4.45, 7.34, and 9.7. Ponder's End at 9.11, 11.15, 12.5, 4.51, 7.40, and 9.14.

Printed and Published by the Proprietor, JOHN HENRY MEYERS, at his Printing Office, at the Public Library, Enfield Town, in the County of Middlesex to whom all communications are to be addressed.

EASTERN COUNTIES' RAILWAY TIME TABLE ZZZ05536 (Enfield Libraries Local History Unit)

ENFIELD AND EDMONTON LOW LEVEL STATIONS

The Enfield Town station building had originally been a house, then a private school. The railway company then converted it to the station without doing much work on it; this was one of the reasons why it was said that the NER had built the line on the cheap (the other was that the line itself was engineered cheaply - it was single track all the way). One of the school's former pupils was the poet John Keats. Nothing remains of this or the subsequent station buildings today. The only reminder is a commemorative plaque, which can been seen inside the booking hall.

ENFIELD TOWN STATION c1849 ZZZ05537
(Enfield Libraries Local History Unit)

ENFIELD TOWN STATION c1945 E179001

THE VICTORIAN ERA

Edmonton Low Level was the second station on the line when it was first built. When Lower Edmonton (Upper Level) was opened the majority of services came through here. Low Level remained mainly as a terminus for the workmen's trains. Like the old Enfield Town station, nothing remains of this station today.

EDMONTON LOW LEVEL STATION c1960
ZZZ05539 (Enfield Libraries Local History Unit)

A TRAIN AT EDMONTON LOW LEVEL STATION c1900 ZZZ05538 (Enfield Libraries Local History Unit)

On this branch there was only one station - Edmonton Low Level. There was a level crossing not long after Water Lane at Jeremys Green Lane (now Montagu Road). Trains leaving Edmonton Low Level then went over another level crossing at Bury Street, then Red Lane (now Lincoln Road), before terminating at Enfield Town. The service had finally reached the Town Centre.

Railway Company was formed in 1862 from several companies, including the Eastern Counties Railway Company.) The line was completed by 1872, and suburban platforms were opened at Liverpool Street in 1874. Enfield Town station was demolished and completely rebuilt. The new line did not signal the end of the low level station at Edmonton, for it was still used as a terminus for some of

THE PLAQUE TO JOHN KEATS 2005 ZZZ05540 (Stephen G Hoye)

This plaque was erected as a tribute to John Keats, the poet. Originally, the Enfield Town station building was the school that Keats attended.

The service along this section of track was unreliable and infrequent. To make matters worse, all services travelled via Stratford. The result of this was that the population of Enfield scarcely grew up to 1850. (However, it expanded vastly in the 20th century; presumably the locals were not concerned at thought of being swamped by multitudes coming from other areas.)

In 1863 the Great Eastern Railway Company obtained an Act of Parliament to build an extension from London to Stoke Newington and then on to Edmonton. (The Great Eastern

the workmen's trains. The line remained into the late 1950s and early 1960s, although it had been closed to passengers since 1939. In fact, the author can still remember trains using the low level station. All that remains now is a footpath that follows the old track bed to Montagu Road. For many years one of the old level crossing gates remained, but that has now disappeared, sad to say.

Up to 1880, after services left Lower Edmonton the next stop had been Enfield Town. After 1880 a new station was built at Bush Hill Park. The hope was that with a

THE VICTORIAN ERA

new estate being built here, the new station would generate more income. It would also save passengers from having to get to either Enfield Town or Lower Edmonton.

Great Eastern's next extension was the construction of a loop between the main line and the Enfield Town line. The loop veered from the Enfield Town line just after the Bury Street level crossing on the right. Stations were put in at Churchbury (now Southbury), Forty Hill (now Turkey Street) and Theobalds Grove. It then rejoined the main line just before Cheshunt. The loop only lasted eighteen years before it was withdrawn because of competition from trams. The First World War was a year old when a special service was reinstated between 1915 and 1919 for munition workers.

Another company, the Great Northern Railway, had obtained an Act of Parliament to build a line from London to Peterborough.

In 1850 the first section to New Southgate and Potters Bar was completed. This included boring two tunnels at Hadley Wood - it seems incredible that they were constructed by navvies using pickaxes and shovels. When the tunnels were bored out, no one thought of putting a station in at Hadley Wood. It was another 35 years before this was done.

The planners within the company then looked for possible branches. A further Act was passed allowing the company to build a branch to Enfield (now Enfield Chase), and the line was completed in 1871; there were stations at Winchmore Hill and Palmers Green. The line stayed this way until 1875, when a further branch was put in. A spur was built from the suburban lines at Finsbury Park to the North London Railway at Canonbury, allowing through running to Broad Street via Dalston Junction. The last piece of the jigsaw

FORTY HILL STATION c1900 ZZZ05541 (Enfield Libraries Local History Unit)

This shows Forty Hill Station, as it was called - today it is known as Turkey Street. It was called Forty Hill because this was probably the nearest point to the station. When the station was opened, the Great Cambridge Road did not exist, and nor did the whole of Turkey Street.

A HISTORY & CELEBRATION

ENFIELD CHASE STATION c1910 ZZZ05542 (Enfield Libraries Local History Unit)

This photograph shows the original Enfield (Enfield Chase) Station. This building was abandoned when the extension was built; it was eventually demolished, and the land was used as sidings. When these were closed, the land was redeveloped into what is now Gladbeck Way.

BUSH HILL STATION, ST MARK'S ROAD c1955 E179036

A rare photograph of Bush Hill Park Station. Note the baker's van on the right, and the milk delivery van just right of centre. The newsagent's on the far right is still there.

THE VICTORIAN ERA

was the building of a station at Bowes Park in 1880; like Great Eastern's building of Bush Hill Park Station, this was due to the building of a new estate. This marked the end of railway development in Enfield in Victoria's reign.

The following table shows the population growth in Edmonton, Enfield and Southgate between 1801 and 1901. These figures are courtesy of LB of Enfield Website, and show the results of the census of the years from 1801 to 1901:

	EDMONTON	ENFIELD	SOUTHGATE
1801	5,095	5,881	
1811	6,824	6,636	
1821	7,900	8,227	
1831	8,192	8,812	(Southgate was part of Edmonton until 1881)
1841	9,027	9,367	
1851	9,708	9,453	
1861	10,930	12,424	
1871	13,860	16,054	
1881	23,436	19,104	
1891	25,361	31,536	10,970
1901	46,899	42,738	14,993

Even with the coming of the railway, the census figures show how little Enfield grew between 1831 and 1851. In the next 30 years the population increased 2.5 times in Enfield and 2 times in Edmonton. To increase population, two things are needed: industry and housing.

On the Edmonton enclosure map (1801) and the Enfield enclosure map (1803), Bush Hill Park is almost completely undeveloped.

There were no houses along the entire length of Lincoln Road. Along the southern fringe was the remote hamlet of Bury Street. At this date the bulk of the land between Bury Street and Lincoln Road was owned by William Mellish. He lived at Bush Hill Park, a large house which stood on the slopes of Bush Hill on a site now occupied by Ringmer Place. Mellish, who came from a Nottinghamshire family, was a director of the Bank of England and Tory MP for Grimsby and later for Middlesex. He died in 1838 and was buried at All Saints' Church, Edmonton. After Mellish's death, the estate passed through several changes of ownership. After being sold in 1871, it was broken up for building land. Development accelerated after 1880 when the Great Eastern Railway opened Bush Hill Park station. (The railway line had been built in 1849.) The first houses in Wellington Road and Village Road went on the market in 1878. The early inhabitants were solidly middle-class, attracted by the large detached houses and the spacious, tree-lined roads. To the east of the railway, development took place on very different lines. Plans were submitted for The Avenues in 1880. The Cardigan Estate was developed in two phases in 1889 and 1892. The area was developed with small terraced houses, and the newcomers were predominantly working-class. The earliest inhabitants included many railway employees: drivers, firemen and guards based at Enfield Town depot.

Cockfosters was a small settlement by 1867, virtually an estate village for Trent Park. Its main component was a collection of cottages

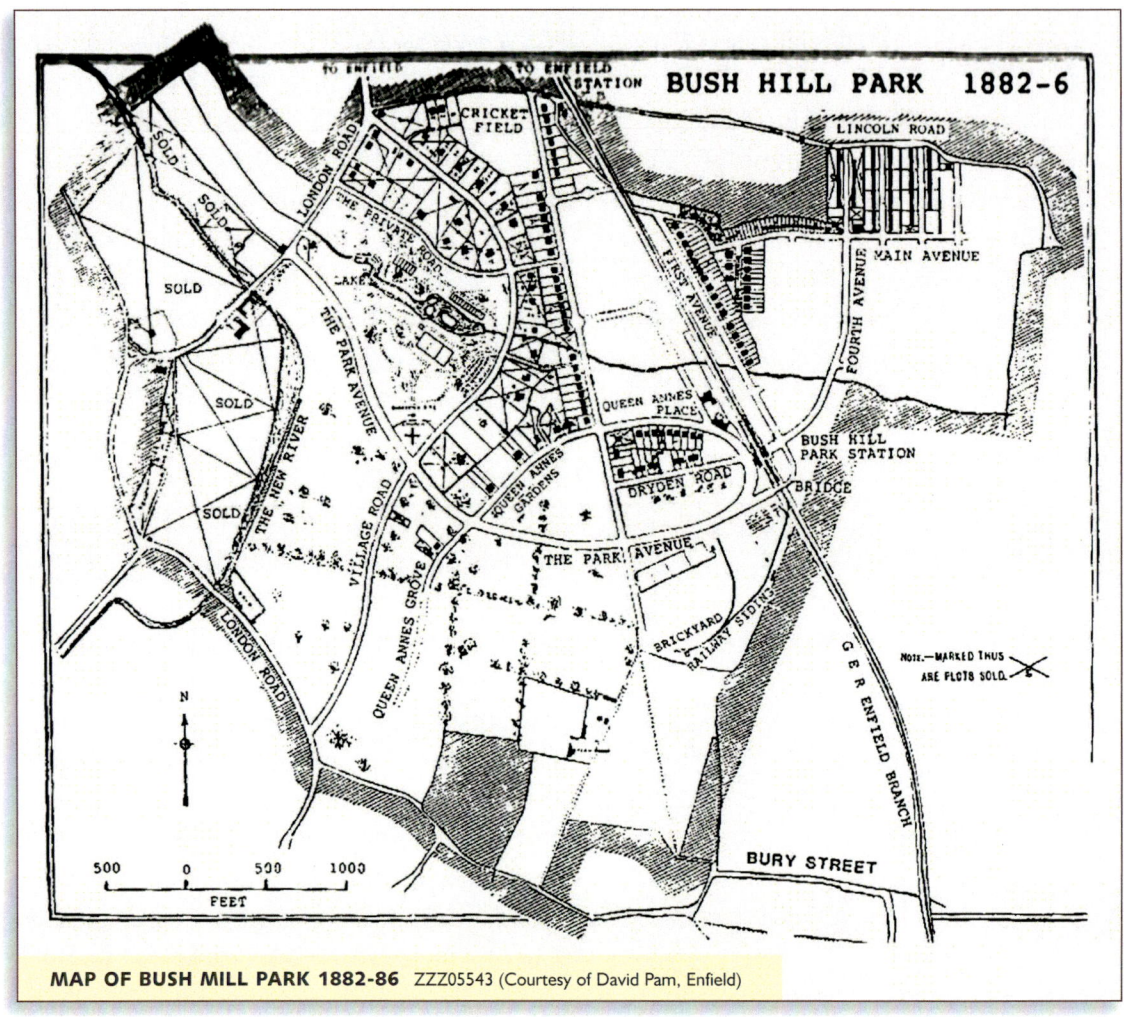

MAP OF BUSH MILL PARK 1882-86 ZZZ05543 (Courtesy of David Pam, Enfield)

This shows the development of Bush Hill Park between 1882 and 1886.

on the west side of Cockfosters Road (north of the main gate to Trent Park). There was a collection of larger houses and a pub (the Cock) in Chalk Lane. Also in Chalk Lane was Christ Church, built in 1839 and paid for by Robert Bevan of Trent Park. (The Bevans, who were partners in Barclays Bank, owned Trent Park from 1833 to 1908.) To the south of Chalk Lane, a row of cottages (Woodside Cottages) lay on the east side of Cockfosters Road at right angles to the road. In the angle between Cockfosters Road and Cat Hill stood Belmont, a substantial house in its own grounds, later known as Heddon Court.

At Hadley Wood, development was at an even more basic level. There were three large houses (West Lodge, Beech Hill Park and Greenwood), plus two small groups of cottages sited on the north side of Camlet Way. There had been no development at

THE VICTORIAN ERA

all in Wagon Road. The Great Northern Railway's main line had been opened in 1850. (The construction involved the boring of two major tunnels.) However, at first no station was provided for Hadley Wood.

> ### Fact File
>
> *When the GNR built the line to Potters Bar, two major tunnels were dug under Hadley Wood, an impressive engineering undertaking that was probably done with pickaxe and shovel.*

In the early 1880s Charles Jack, the owner of Beech Hill Park, drew up plans to develop much of Hadley Wood. In 1882 he signed a building lease with the Duchy of Lancaster to lay out streets and build houses. Negotiations with the Great Northern Railway resulted in the opening of a station at Hadley Wood in 1885. By 1896 Crescent Road (later Crescent East and Crescent West) was partly built up. Some large detached houses had appeared on the north side of Beech Hill. Lancaster Avenue had been laid out, but was as yet without houses. By 1914, apart from the addition of a few houses in Lancaster Avenue, Hadley Wood had grown relatively little.

Eastern Enfield had grown sufficiently by 1831 to justify its own parish church (St James's). Much of the early housing development was directly linked with the housing needs of the Royal Small Arms Factory. In the angle between Ordnance Road and Hertford Road, Grove Road and Alma Road (both now demolished) were developed from the mid 1850s. Medcalf Road and Warwick Road were built in the early 1860s. The Putney Lodge Estate (including Mandeville Road and Totteridge Road) was developed from 1867.

Upper Edmonton started life as a hamlet centred on the intersection of Fore Street with Silver Street and Water Lane (Angel Road). By the early 19th century it had been extended by ribbon development along Fore Street until it formed a long straggling settlement stretching from the Tottenham boundary to just south of Boards' Lane (Brettenham Road). By the mid 1860s, further ribbon development was closing the gap between Upper and Lower Edmonton. At this time Upper Edmonton must have looked very like some of the single street villages so common in Hertfordshire.

Lower Edmonton is shown on the enclosure map of 1801 as a well-established settlement. The centre was situated where the main turnpike road widened out to form Edmonton Green. Salmon's Brook, after winding its way eastwards from Bush Hill, crossed the Green, spreading out to form a large pool. Northwards, the settlement extended along the Hertford Road to just north of the junction with Town Lane (Town Road). Southwards, there was patchy development along Fore Street stretching just beyond the junction with Knight's Lane. Westwards, Church Street was built up to a point just beyond All Saints' Church, and there were a few houses in Church lane and Milestone Alley (Victoria Road). The 25-inch to the mile Ordnance Survey map of 1867 shows a limited amount of growth. Some large villas had been built in Church Street, and ribbon development along Fore Street had almost reached Boards' Lane (Brettenham Road), virtually closing the gap between Upper and Lower Edmonton.

Enfield Town's suburban development began shortly after the opening of the first railway station in 1849. The first major development was Enfield New Town (Raleigh Road, Essex Road, Sydney Road and Cecil Road), which was built up from 1852. This was a mixed development with large houses in London Road and Essex Road and small workmen's cottages in Sydney Road and Raleigh Road. To the east of Chase Side the Gordon House Estate was developed slowly from 1858. In the Lancaster Road area the Woodlands Estate, the Cedars Estate and the Birkbeck Estate were all developed from the late 1870s. The Windmill Hill area saw some up-market housing developments. The Bycullah Estate (1878), the Old Park Estate (1880) and the Glebe Estate (1880) were all distinctly high-class developments, consisting mainly of large detached houses.

> ### Fact File
> The Crown and Horseshoes public house at the end of Parsonage Gardens has a ghost, a lady who has been seen in the cellar.

CHURCH STREET c1950 E179007

It must be a Saturday, since there are so many people around. Note that traffic is two-way. The clock on the left-hand side is not there now.

Forty Hill had changed relatively little since 1572: by the mid 19th century its layout and the disposition of the settlements were much as they had always been. Being remote from public transport, the area was unattractive to commuters and grew relatively little. In 1868 the Bridgen Hall Estate was sold for building - this was a large tract of land between Carterhatch Lane and Goat Lane. The streets were laid out: St George's Road, Garnault Road, Russell Road, Layard Road and Bridgenhall Road. Development, mainly in the form of workmen's cottages, was extremely slow and protracted. There were vacant plots on this estate well into the 1930s. In addition, gravel digging took place on parts of the estate, which resulted in subsidence problems in the mid 20th century.

THE VICTORIAN ERA

On the other hand, New Southgate's core had been built up by 1867; this was a triangular area bounded by the High Road, Palmers Green Road (now Palmers Road) and Bowes Road. The area was originally solidly middle-class, but it soon begun to acquire a shabby-genteel flavour. This phenomenon was associated with the presence of the Colney Hatch Asylum. The very name Colney Hatch became synonymous with mental illness, which seriously impeded the development of the area.

In 1867, Palmers Green was the kind of village that you would miss if you blinked whilst you passed through. It had a public

THE GEORGE INN c1860 ZZZ05544 (Enfield Libraries Local History Unit)

The public house is the George - note the arch where the coaches and horses used to go in and out. The shop next door is Meyer's, then just a printer and bookseller, but later to become the first proprietor of the Enfield Gazette and Observer.

house, the Fox, and a few cottages where Fox Lane and Hazelwood Lane join Green Lanes. South of this lay another small hamlet called Bowes, in the area around the Cock Tavern. At the junction of Fox Lane and Dog and Duck Lane (now Bourne Hill) was Clappers Green. The land on which these hamlets or villages stood was owned by the then big estates of the area: Grovelands, Broomfield, Bowes Manor, and The Lodge. When the Great Northern Railway opened its branch line from Wood Green to Enfield in 1881, Palmers Green station was built. The major problem was that the station was in open country - the

SOUTHGATE, THE GREEN c1955 S641048

This looks like a quiet English village green. Note the water trough for horses in the foreground.

WINCHMORE HILL, GROVELANDS PARK c1955
W482009

SOUTHGATE, GROVELANDS PARK HOUSE c1955
S641017

nearest houses were nearly a quarter of a mile away near the Fox. This must have been very disconcerting for passengers alighting here, especially those who were new to the area. The major landowners held on to their land and would not sell; it is thanks to this that very little development took place over a period of around 30 years. The only buildings that did appear were large village villas between Fox Lane and Hoppers Road on the west side of Green Lanes, erected in 1896. These villas still stand today; one is now the HQ for the Bureau of Freelance Photographers.

Ponders End's housing development began at a fairly early date. Alma Road was developed from 1855, and Napier Road had been laid out by 1867. The Lincoln House Estate (Derby Road and Lincoln Road) was built up from 1871. Durants Road was developed from 1888 and Nags Head Road from 1890.

Southgate's first attempt at suburban development dates from 1853. A large tract of land bounded by Chase Side, Chase Road and Bramley Road was sold for building. Streets were laid out: Avenue Road, Nursery Road, Reservoir Road, Chelmsford Road, and

THE VICTORIAN ERA

so on. Some workmen's cottages were erected in Chelmsford Road and Nursery Road, while a few larger houses went up in Chase Side and parts of Avenue Road and Chase Road. The builders had great difficulty in finding tenants for the houses, and work ground to a halt.

Industry within the borough during the Victorian period was mainly focused on the Royal Small Arms Factory. The bringing together of these workers not only helped the economy of the country, but also meant that an organisation to assist them was created, the Enfield Co-operative Society. The Co-op would grow into a very large organisation - not only was it a retailer, but it was an insurer, financier, and social organisation as well. It is sad that the number of stores has been reduced by a take-over. Enfield had two stores, one in London Road and one in Lancaster Road; now only the latter remains.

For a brief period (its final year of trading was 1894) there was a crepe mill in Enfield, owned by Grout & Baylis; they made black crepe, a silk fabric very much in demand for mourning clothes.

The oldest industry, which still survives today, is Wright's flour mill. The present buildings date from the late 18th century, but there has been a mill on the site since at least the late 16th century, and possibly since Domesday. George Reynolds Wright was born at Hitchin in 1842. At the age of 25 he came to work at the Ponders End Mill, and he eventually formed a partnership with the then miller, James Dilly Young. On Young's death in 1870, Wright assumed full control. In 1913 construction work on the

SOUTHGATE, ARLINGTON ROAD c1955 S641031

This is one of Southgate's suburban developments.

43

A History & Celebration

George V Reservoir cut off the water supply which powered the millstones, and so the machinery was converted to electric power. The mill was re-modelled in 1950, and there have been further improvements since then. The business remains in the hands of the Wright family.

> ### Fact File
>
> *From the early part of 19th century to the late 1970s there was a brick works in Enfield at Hoe Lane. This is an unexpected industry for this part of the world - we normally associate brick making with Bedfordshire.*

Another short-lived company opened a jute mill. Jute is a long, soft, shiny fibre that can be spun into coarse, strong threads. It is one of the cheapest natural fibres, and is second only to cotton in the amount produced and the variety of uses it can be put to. Jute is used chiefly to make cloth for wrapping bales of raw cotton, and to make gunny sacks and gunny cloth. The fibres are also woven into curtains, chair coverings, carpets, and burlap. Very fine threads of jute are made into imitation silk. The fibres are used alone or blended with other types of fibres to make twine and rope. Jute butts, the coarse ends of the plants, are used to make inexpensive cloth. The company lasted only from 1859 to 1886, but the trade of jute weaver was mentioned in the 1901 census.

EDMONTON ZZZ05546
(Enfield Libraries Local History Unit)

EDMONTON GREEN ZZZ05547
(Enfield Libraries Local History Unit)

THE VICTORIAN ERA

POOR SOCIAL CONDITIONS IN THE 1850s

A report by the General Board of Health (1850) on sanitary conditions in Edmonton reveals a very sorry state of affairs (indeed, the photographs of Edmonton show that the area was poorer than other parts). Pymmes Brook was little better than an open sewer, and there had been an outbreak of typhus in a common lodging house in Orchard Street (Raynham Road). The 1851 census reveals evidence of gross overcrowding in the area, including several lodging houses that were largely populated by refugees from the Irish potato famine. As for Lower Edmonton, there was an outbreak of typhus in Church Lane and bad drainage in Barrowfield Lane, but this was nothing to what Upper Edmonton went through. The General Board of Health also reported on sanitary conditions in Enfield. It revealed an alarming state of affairs in Ponders End: many of the older cottages were grossly overcrowded and extremely unsanitary - the worst affected areas were South Street and Scotland Green. The whole area suffered from poor drainage.

EDMONTON, THE CROSS KEYS ZZZ05545 (Enfield Libraries Local History Unit)

The company that took over the mill was founded by two separate individuals who discovered the same thing. These were Thomas Edison and Joseph Swan, who both developed the electric light filament. Swan saw the potential of his invention, and started a factory in Newcastle in 1881. Two years later Swan and Edison joined forces to form the Edison Swan Co Ltd in Benwell, Newcastle. Three years later in 1886 they took over the old jute mill, and so began a long-lived and prosperous business. The company was eventually taken over, and is now part of Marconi plc.

Other major industries which were born in the mid to latter part of the 19th century were the Edmonton gasworks in 1847 and Ponders End gasworks in 1859. Agriculture was important too; for much of the century, the marshes around the River Lea were excellent grazing lands. Some of the lanes to the marshes are still in existence today, including Stockingswater Lane, Millmarsh Lane, Bell Lane, and Pigots Lane (now known as Carterhatch Road).

With the increase in population, the development of industry, and the new housing that was being built, many social issues came to the fore: more schools were needed, along with proper drainage and sewage systems, wholesome drinking water, and a gas supply for domestic and street lighting.

In 1855, under the powers of the Public Health Act of 1848, the Local Board of Health, who were the front runners of the UDC, set up Enfield Waterworks. This comprised a well and pumping station in Alma Road, Ponders End; a reservoir on Holtwhites Hill; and an extra well sunk behind Eagle House in Ponders End High Street. The eastern side of Enfield was served by a reservoir which was built on land on the north side of Southbury Road. In 1894 Enfield Waterworks acquired the Bycullah Waterworks, which had been set up to cover the new estate. It was situated in Rowantree Road, and was still functioning as late as 1923. Other areas in Enfield were served by different water companies such as the New River Company in Bush Hill Park (which was the oldest), the Barnet Gas and Water Company which took care of Cockfosters and Hadley Wood, and the North Middlesex Company which looked after New Southgate. Many of these companies did not last long on their own, as they were acquired one by one by the Metropolitan Water Board in 1904.

Another aspect of the increase in population was that more schools were needed, and more churches too - church attendance was far more widespread in Victorian times, even among the working class. In the period up to 1901, 20 schools and nine churches were built and opened.

The latter half of the 19th century saw several other pieces of the welfare jigsaw put in place. Although each may be insignificant on its own, to the people of Enfield each was a source of benefit. The Edmonton Poor Law Union was set up in 1837, covering the parishes of Hampstead, Hornsey, Tottenham, Edmonton, Enfield,

THE VICTORIAN ERA

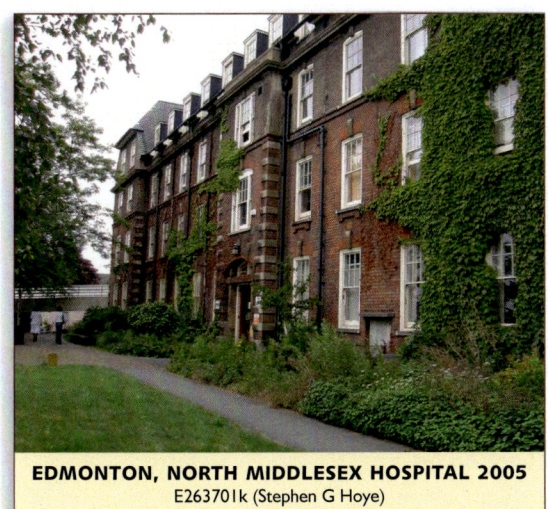

EDMONTON, NORTH MIDDLESEX HOSPITAL 2005
E263701k (Stephen G Hoye)

Not much of the old workhouse is still extant; these buildings, which are now offices and clinics, are probably part of the remnants.

Chestnut and Waltham Abbey. A new Edmonton Union workhouse was erected in Silver Street, and opened in 1842 for able bodied paupers. The site is now occupied by North Middlesex Hospital. Photograph E263701k (above) shows some of the original buildings.

From the time of the Domesday Book, Southgate had been part of Edmonton; in 1881 it finally became an entity in its own right. In 1885 Highlands Hospital was begun; it was eventually completed in 1890, and served as an isolation unit. A Poor Law Orphanage was opened at Chase Farm (now Chase Farm Hospital), the year 1886.

In 1889, Middlesex County Council came into being. Previously all decisions county-wide had been made by judges at quarter sessions. Six years later, a more distinguishable form of local government started. All three parishes lost their Local Boards of Health. Instead, each parish became an Urban District Council. This had been made possible by the implementation of the 1894 Local Government Act. Also established at the same time under the terms of the 1870 Education Act was the Enfield School Board, which oversaw the running of all the schools in the area.

As the Victorian area came to a close in 1901, each area was in a state of transition from being a rural community to being an urban one. Further change was bound to come during the 20th century.

Fact File

Charles Lamb, the essayist (1775-1834), lived in Enfield on Gentleman's Row. There is also a building named after him in Church Street, Edmonton.

CHARLES LAMB'S HOUSE 2005
ZZZ05548 (Stephen G Hoye)

The house that Charles Lamb lived in is the one immediately on the right.

47

ENFIELD
A HISTORY & CELEBRATION

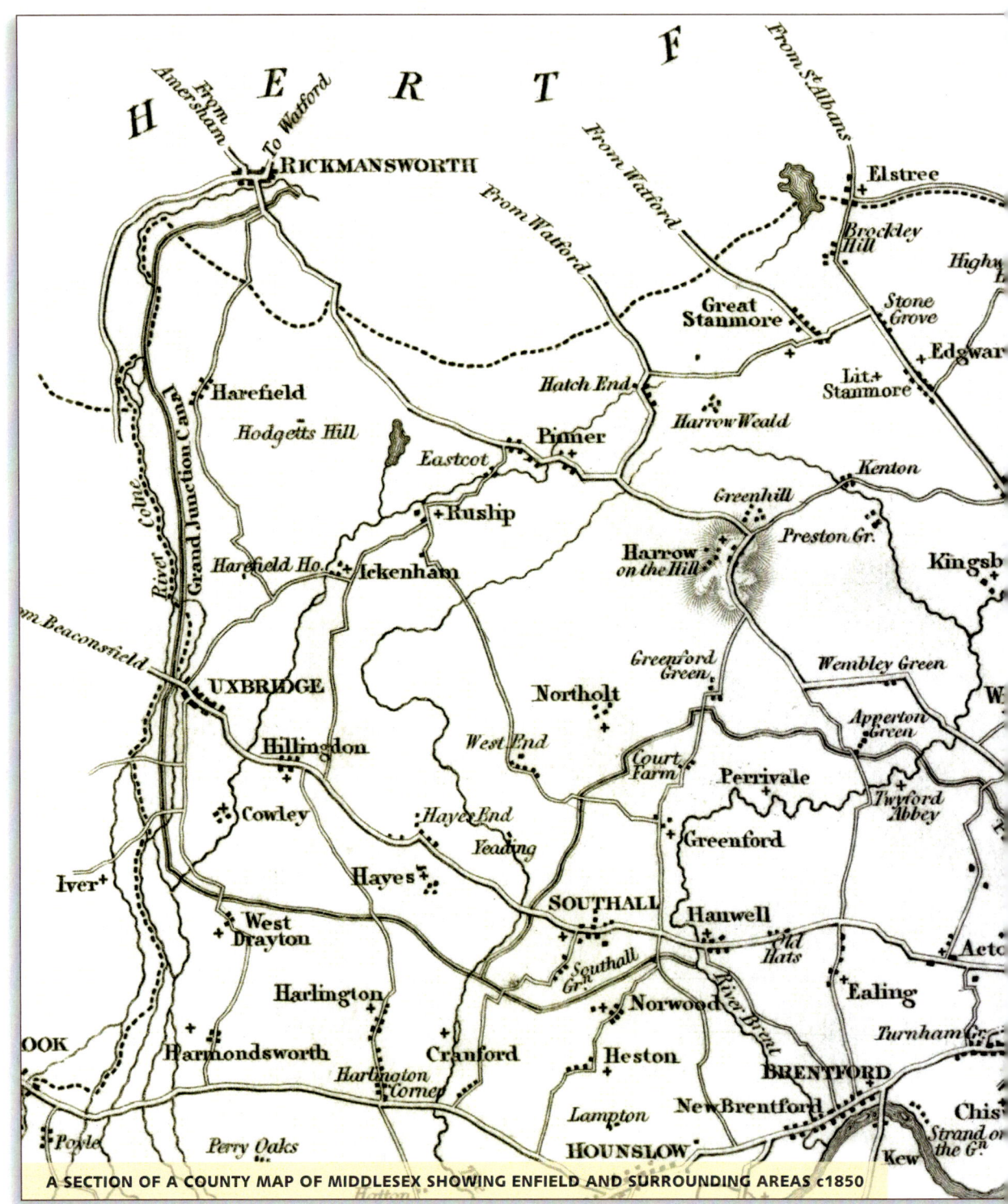

A SECTION OF A COUNTY MAP OF MIDDLESEX SHOWING ENFIELD AND SURROUNDING AREAS c1850

ENFIELD COUNTY MAP

CHAPTER THREE
EARLY MODERNISATION

ENFIELD
A HISTORY & CELEBRATION

FORTY HILL c1955 F186001

There had been a lot of development in the Enfield area from the 1850s onwards, and the end of Victoria's reign did not put a stop to it. One of the legacies that the Victorian era did leave us with was that the standard of construction was very good - indeed, the builders of that era deserve more credit than they have been given. This can be seen in some of the estates around the area.

Bush Hill Park's development continued uninterrupted until the First World War. Park Avenue seems to have been used a guide to the building in the Bush Hill Park area. Queen Anne's Gardens, Dryden Road, and Wellington Road had been built to the north. The area to the south, which included Edenbridge and Bagshot Roads and the next part of Wellington Road, were laid out, but no work was started - the probable reason for this was that this was 1914, the year the war started. Following the First World War, building resumed on what was called the New River Estate. Here each avenue was named after a place in Kent: Sittingbourne, Faversham, Teynham and Borden. The first houses were occupied by 1926, and by 1935 Bush Hill Park was fully developed.

By 1914 Cockfosters had grown relatively little, apart from the addition of a few houses in Lancaster Avenue. The Ordnance Survey map for that year showed that, in comparison to other areas, Cockfosters had

EARLY MODERNISATION

hardly altered since 1867. There were two changes, in that Ludgrove and Heddon Court had become boys' preparatory schools. Trent Park, which had been owned by the late Sir Edward Sassoon, had undergone a complete overhaul, instigated by Sir Philip, son of the former owner, and socialites gathered here to enjoy elaborate parties. There were abortive attempts to break the estates up, but the only one to change was Beech Hill in 1922, where part of the land became a golf course, with the old house becoming the clubhouse. By 1939 Cockfosters and its surrounding environs was a suburban enclave.

At the turn of the century, eastern Enfield (excluding Ponders End, which will be discussed separately) was a rapidly growing district. Off Ordnance Road, building had begun just before 1900, and continued up to the First World War. The roads being

THE WRECKED ZEPPELIN AT CUFFLEY 1916 ZZZ05549 (Enfield Libraries Local History Unit)

The photograph shows men from the army retrieving the pieces from the Zeppelin shot down over Cuffley.

developed were Beaconsfield Road, Catisfield Road and Chesterfield Road, with some additional neighbouring roads. It was not until the period between the wars that the Rosary Estate became completely urbanised. Further up the Hertford Road, development was taking place on the old Freezywater Farm. Once completed, this part of Enfield kept Freezywater as the local name for the district.

Between Brimsdown Station and Ordnance Road on the east side of the Hertford Road, building had been spasmodic. The ten years before 1900 had seen some building, but there was room for more. Albany Road and St Stephens Road had been started - these two roads were completed in the early years of the 20th century. Comments had been made that Enfield Highway needed more artisans' houses to complement the good service of workmen's trains from Enfield Lock. Seeing that the population on this side of Enfield was increasing, the UDC opened Albany Park for public use in 1902 (the cost was £3,937, the equivalent of £262,000 today) and Durants Park in 1903. Enfield Town Park was bought in 1903 for £6,750 (the equivalent of £443,000) and Hilly Fields in 1911 for £7,950 (£495,000). These figures come from Graham Dalling's book 'Enfield Past'.

With more people came the need for more shops. Some buildings which had originally been housing were considered ideal for this purpose, and a gradual replacement took place. After the lean years for house building in the 1920s, between 1931 and 1937 further building took place. In these six years planning permission was given for the building of 21 estates totalling 2,500 homes. A possible stimulus for this building, the Great Cambridge Road, had been open for seven years. The UDC also undertook the building of two council estates, these were the Albany and the Suffolk estates. The table shows which roads belonged to which estate:

ALBANY	SUFFOLK
Brimsdown Avenue	Central Avenue
Croft Road	The Approach
Meads Road	Brick Lane
Castle Road	Wolsey Road
Redlands Road	Barnard Road
Lee Road	Gough Road
The Link	Tyberry Road
	Broadfield Square
	Mapleton Road
	Hammond Road

The period before and after the First World War was one of further development for Edmonton, with the emphasis on the working class. Families from the inner London suburbs had been attracted to the district by both the housing and the cheap workmen's tickets offered by the railway. By the outbreak of war, large tracts of land had been built over; these included the considerable development along the Hertford Road in Bounces Road, Bury Street, and Victoria Road. After the First World War the first council estate for Edmonton was built to the west of Victoria Road. The Church Street area, on the other hand, saw a lot of private building. These were large houses with three or four floors along with compact terraced housing. All this

EARLY MODERNISATION

WINCHMORE HILL, THE NEW RIVER AND THE CRICKET GROUND c1960 W482034

There is not a cricketer in sight!

development was like ivy, creeping gradually until the area was completely covered. The southern half of the district was generally already in a well-developed state. It was the mid 1930s when the last tract of land was built upon. This was the Dyson's estate, which saw the area from Middleham Road to the North Circular Road totally developed.

It was a different story altogether in Southgate. There had been very little development of the area in the 19th century. That started to change as early as 1902, when the Grovelands Estate was sold in lots after the last owner, Major R K Taylor, had died; this reversed a previous decision to make the estate into a private green belt. However, before the sale went through, a part of the estate was withdrawn.

WINCHMORE HILL, THE GREEN c1960 W482047

By this date there are a few more cars in this pleasant scene.

A HISTORY & CELEBRATION

SOUTHGATE, GROVELANDS PARK GATES c1955 S641013

Note the gas lamp on the right hand side of this photograph. In 1911 64 acres of the grounds of the Grovelands Estate were purchased by Southgate Urban District Council for a public park. Grovelands Park was officially opened on 12 April 1913. It is now on the register of Historic Parks and Gardens.

ADVERTISEMENT FOR ULLESWATER ROAD ESTATE
ZZZ05551 (Enfield Libraries Local History Unit)

The area was bounded by Grovelands, The Bourne, Winchmore Hill Road, Church Hill and the railway. It is during this early period before the First World War that the district began to take shape. It appears that 1905 was one of the big years for building - at this time there were 645 planning applications covering roads in New Southgate, Palmers Green, and Winchmore Hill. The number of builders involved was 40. It should be noted here that in one of the roads, Ulleswater Road, the builder W J Edwards had priced his houses from £375 to £1,400, the equivalent in today's prices of £126,905 to £473,778. Of these 645 planning applications, many were made by builders for just three or four houses, and the smallest application was for one house.

EARLY MODERNISATION

ADVERTISEMENT FOR OLD PARK GRANGE ESTATE
ZZZ05550 (Enfield Libraries Local History Unit)

Enfield Town and its surrounding environs began to take shape at the turn of the century. Around The Ridgeway and its associated roads, including Holtwhites Hill, Uplands Park Road, and Slades Hill, some fine housing had been built at the end of the century. Drapers Road had been laid out, but no building had taken place - no house was built there until after 1920.

Enfield Town itself was more or less as it is today. The George, which perhaps had always been a focal point, had been knocked down and rebuilt in 1911. Most of the older shops had been knocked down and rebuilt as well. Included in this rebuilding was a new shopping area known as Town Parade at the beginning of Silver Street. The western side of the market place started to change dramatically when the former Burleigh House was sold in 1913 - this was on the north side of Church Street. The development included shops and a cinema.

SOUTHGATE, WINCHMORE HILL ROAD c1955 S641024

ENFIELD
A HISTORY & CELEBRATION

THE POST OFFICE 2005 ZZZ05555 (Stephen G Hoye)

This is the top of the post office building; the coat of arms is the royal coat of arms.

The south side of Church Street began its facelift when the manor house was demolished in 1928. Pearsons, who had taken over Lock's Drapery Store in 1902, had taken over the site when the palace was demolished, and had a purpose-built shop erected in its place. That shop is still there today - it is one of the few shops left of those built at that time, and it is still trading. Another, the author believes, is Berndes fish shop. The post office had opened for business in Church Street in 1906.

There was extensive building on both sides of Southbury Road in the immediate period before the First World War; the land had been mostly market gardens up until then. A recreation ground was created from this land, called Bush Hill Park, bounded

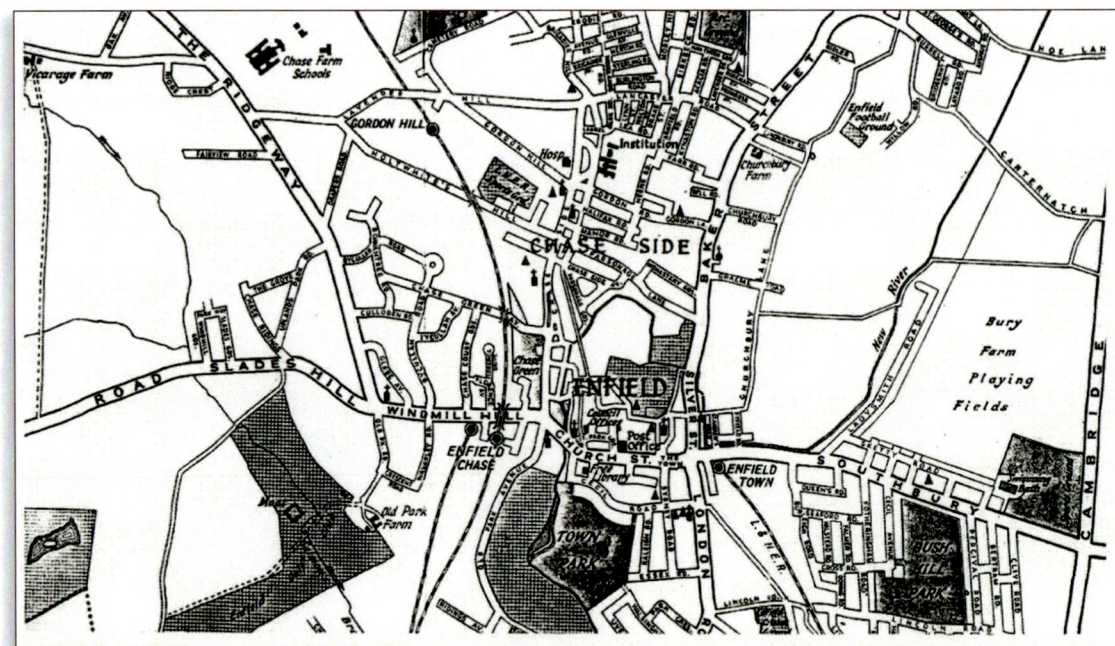

Map showing Enfield Town and the surrounding area in the mid-thirties. None of the respectable estates which now cover the former fields between Baker Street and the New River had yet been built. Enfield football ground at Cherry Lane and Churchbury Farm are shown.

A MAP SHOWING ENFIELD TOWN IN THE 1930s ZZZ05556 (Courtesy of David Pam, Enfield)

EARLY MODERNISATION

by Lincoln and Southbury Roads. The other streets in this little estate have Welsh names: Craddock (the actual Welsh is Caradoc), Clydach, Sketty, and Bryn-y-mawr.

The opening of the Great Cambridge Road in 1923/24 did stimulate some building, though not so much around Enfield Town.

> **Fact File**
>
> It was in 1903 that Enfield created Town Park from the grounds of Chaseside House. This was the first of several public parks proposed by the UDC.

Some council houses were built, but it was mostly private housing that went up. Monastery Gardens, Churchbury Lane and Baker Street were the areas where the development was carried out. In total, permission had been granted to build 1159 new homes.

Ponders End appears to have been a slow developer. Streets here had been planned before 1900, but the actual development only gained momentum later. There were small pockets in Nags Head Road, Lincoln Road and to the south of South Street, which was on the old Allens Farm, but this last area only fully realized its potential in the 1930s. On the west side of the Hertford Road (the part called Ponders End High Street), Northfield Road, Southfield Road and Clarence Road

ENFIELD POLICE STATION 1909 ZZZ05554 (Enfield Libraries Local History Unit)

The police remained here until the new station was opened in 1965. The building remained until the early 1980s, when it was demolished and an office block built in its place.

were developed. Further over, Norfolk Road, Suffolk Road and Oxford Road swallowed another piece of farmland. North of Nags Head Road, progress and a bigger population meant that Durants Road, Alexandra Road (named after Queen Alexandra), and King Edward's Road (named after Edward VII, not the potato) joined all the others on

SOUTHGATE, THE MINCHENDEN OAK GARDENS c1955 S641052

The Minchenden Oak Gardens were created as an evergreen Garden of Remembrance, opened in 1934.

SOUTHGATE, THE MINCHENDEN OAK c1955
S641051

The Minchenden Oak grows in the grounds of the gardens.

the map. There is one estate that is hardly ever mentioned: this is the Welsh Estate, developed between 1921 and 1925. The author's mother and her sister grew up on this estate, and went to school just round the corner. The roads involved were Brecon Road, Tenby Road, Aberdare Road, Anglesey Road and Cardiff Road.

By the turn of the century, industry had started to flourish. There were already some

EARLY MODERNISATION

> **Fact File**
>
> Halliwick House, which was demolished in 1993, was once the residence of Sir Samuel Cunard, the founder of the Cunard Line shipping company.

notable firms here, as well as the Small Arms Factory. Ediswan, who had moved to Enfield before 1900, made a break-through before 1910 in producing the first thermonic radio valve (a device to amplify a signal). By 1916 the company was producing radio valves commercially. The company was eventually taken over by Thorn's. Ediswan had by this time converted to producing television tubes.

Another notable company was the Flexible Tubing Company. They had started just before 1900, having taken over the old premises of Baylis & Grout, who made the crepe - the works were on the corner of South Street and Scotland Green Road. Flexible Tubing's product had been developed in France. The company had presumably seen its potential and either copied the way it was made or bought the rights to it - no exact information is available. By 1900 and in the years after, the railways had developed steam brakes for locomotives along with vacuum and Westinghouse brakes for rolling stock; these all required flexible hoses. Soon there were other industries requiring flexible hoses too.

With the power station at Brimsdown going live in 1907, this started attracting more heavy industry. Besides the power generated here, there was the additional incentive that there was plenty of space available alongside the River Lea. The following table shows the companies who came here after 1900 and their locations:

It is a sad fact that of these companies only

1900	Ashby Plating	Colmore Rd
1901	Thomas Morson	Brimsdown
1910	Ruberoid	Brimsdown
1913	Imperial Lamp Works	Brimsdown
	Brimsdown Lead Works	Brimsdown
	Enfield Standard Cables	Brimsdown
1921	Paper Factory	Alma Road
1924	Enfield Rolling Mills	Brimsdown
	Electric Smelting Works	Brimsdown
1928	Brimsdown Castings	Brimsdown
1935	Enfield Tool	Aden Road
1937	Slicing Machine Works	Alma Road
1943	Barton's Forge & Iron Works	Aden Road
	Alexandra Works	Brimsdown

two remain. The others have either fallen by the wayside or have been swallowed up by large corporations, and these factories have closed. The building of the Great Cambridge Road opened the way for industry to take over what had previously been market gardens; all the development took place on the east side of the Great Cambridge Road between Southbury Road and Carterhatch

A HISTORY & CELEBRATION

Lane. The companies that started here were Belling & Lee, Sangamo Weston, Ford, Symonds, Sydney Bird, Mays, Cosmocord, Artofex and Sylvan Works. On the other side of Southbury Road, the land remained untouched. In Southbury Road only one company was operating. This was Belling's, who made electric fires and cookers. They took up about half of the area. On the other side of the road the brickworks remained.

In the 1930s some industry grew up in The Queensway, Ponders End. Some of these firms were involved in electrical component manufacture; others, like English Numbering Machines, made parts to go in fruit machines and stamping machines. Stadium Ltd made plastic components, and at one time were known for their motorcycle helmets.

Industry in Lower Edmonton developed along the Hertford Road, mostly towards Enfield along the railway line - at one time there were sawmills around the Green. Industrial growth really occurred between the 1920s and 1930s. Chichester Road, which was one of the new roads, had a slipper factory, and the same type of business was also going on in Rosebery Road. By today's standards, the business in Rosebery Road would have raised a few eyebrows, as the factory was built on land reserved for housing. Small industrial firms were also trading in Brettenham Road (which is south along Fore Street about half-way down on the left-hand side); in the 1920s there were three firms here, and in the 1930s there were eight.

In Upper Edmonton and the Palmers Green side of Southgate two names really stand out. These are MK Electric and Metal

WINCHMORE HILL, THE GREEN DRAGON c1960 W482045

Note the absence of traffic. An Austin A35 van is parked on the left.

EARLY MODERNISATION

THE EARLY LONDON TRAMS

These three photographs show the early varieties of London Tram. The top left is actually horse-drawn.
It was not until the opening of the power station that the trams were converted to run on a single overhead wire. The later trams were bigger, and fully enclosed to keep the public dry.
The trams in these photographs all date from 1890 through to 1910.

EARLY LONDON TRAMS ZZZ05557 (Enfield Libraries Local History Unit)

Box, which both had sizeable works in the area. MK had started in 1919, and Metal Box in 1929. Other industrial development occurred in the Angel Road by the River Lea. One company here, Aerators, was formed in 1901, when they purchased a three-acre site; the company's name may be unknown to most people, but they manufacture a well-known product: Sparklets, the bulbs that put the fizz into drinks. During the First World War the company turned to munitions, and extended its premises and increased the workforce. At the cessation of hostilities the company downsized, and sold some of site to British Oxygen. When Angel Road became part of the North Circular Road, the number of companies here increased from 8 in 1926 to 37 in 1937.

A HISTORY & CELEBRATION

ENFIELD, VILLAGE ROAD c1955 E179034

Those were the days when cycling was safe. Note the tram wires going from pole to pole.

Transport in the borough continued to improve. The trams, which had now been converted to run on a single overhead wire, were already running to Wood Green and Tottenham, and in 1905 the service was extended to Edmonton. It is here that Tramway Avenue comes into the picture and begins its long association with the area and with local public transport. It had started life before 1900, but it was completely remodelled by the tram company when operations began in 1905. The following year Tramway Avenue became just another garage and a crew change point. In this year the tram company extended the service as far as Freezywater, then two years later in 1908 to Waltham Cross.

A bus depot was built at Palmers Green next to the Cock public house. This garage was used for buses which served the area; it was opened in July 1912, and still stands in the same place today. In 1911 a service began from Ponders End to Enfield Town via Southbury road. The author's parents both recalled taking this journey many times; the trams, they said, were extremely uncomfortable, and they seemed to bounce along the road. The route number was 49A, and this service was

EARLY MODERNISATION

TRAM SERVICE EXPANSION

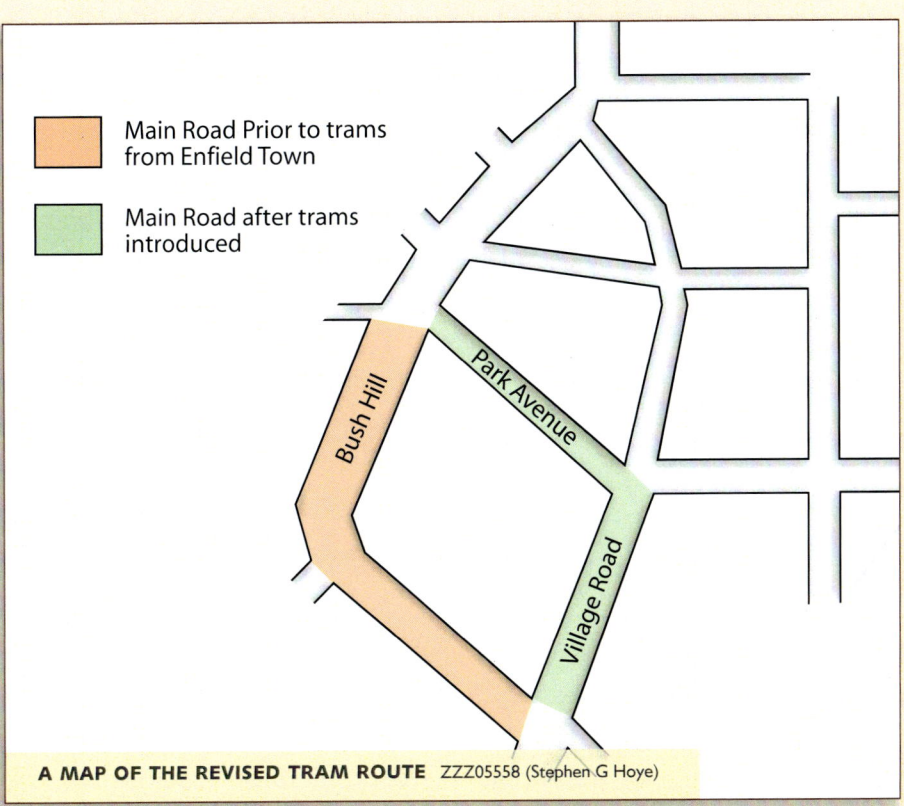

A MAP OF THE REVISED TRAM ROUTE ZZZ05558 (Stephen G Hoye)

The Metropolitan Electric Tram Company, who eventually controlled most of northern North London, acquired the service that was terminating at Wood Green and built an extension up to the Green Dragon, Winchmore Hill in 1907. It would be another two years before the service reached Enfield Town. The delay was due to the need to construct the rails and power lines and modify the roads. Up to the time when the track was laid, the through road from Enfield to Winchmore Hill led over Bush Hill, down Bush Hill Road, and then along Ridge Avenue. When the tramlines were being laid it was realised that they could not negotiate this route. It was then agreed to change the route by going along Park Avenue from London Road to St Stephen's Church and then along Village Road to rejoin the crossroads. The map shows the original main road and the revised route for the trams. This never changed, as the trolleybuses needed the extra space.

just between Ponders End and Enfield. Other services were:

21	North Finchley to Holborn
27	Edmonton Town Hall to Tottenham Court Road
29	Enfield Town to Tottenham Court Road
39A	Enfield Town to Bruce Grove via Wood Green
41	Winchmore Hill to Moorgate
49	Edmonton Town Hall to Liverpool Street Station
59	Waltham Cross to Holborn
79	Waltham Cross to Smithfield Market

As for each of the other UDCs, Edmonton was well covered, but there was no service into Southgate. A service was installed from Bounds Green to New Southgate in 1907, and this was then extended to North Finchley in 1909.

In 1927 the London General Omnibus Company realised that there was a need for another garage, and built one at Ponders End. They handed over it over to the London Public Omnibus Company for their use. Further land was acquired in 1930 for a forecourt, which was used as a terminus. The LPOC was wound up, and its affairs taken over by the London Transport Passenger Board. But this garage housed and still houses buses serving the local area.

In 1933 the London Transport Passenger Board amalgamated all the various companies into one body. The following year a decision was taken to replace the trams with trolleybuses. This was done because the trams were getting old, and servicing was a problem. It was another four years before the changeover took place and another phase of London public transport passed into history. In Enfield each of the tram routes except one was taken over by trolleybuses. The only route that did not change over to trolleybuses was the one from Ponders End up Southbury Road to Enfield Town, where the trams were replaced by motor buses. The new routes were:

521	North Finchley to Holborn
621	North Finchley to Holborn
627	Waltham Cross to Tottenham Court Road
629	Enfield to Tottenham Court Road
641	Winchmore Hill to Moorgate
649	Ponders End to Liverpool Street (extended in the early mornings to Waltham Cross)
659	Waltham Cross to Holborn
679	Waltham Cross to Smithfield

The trolleybuses then carried the weight of London services from 1938. There were also ordinary motor buses which served all areas. If we look at a bus map for 1940, we can see that there about eight or nine routes that are still the same now as they were then. One other small point is that the trolleybus route numbers were formed by putting a 6 in front of the tram route numbers; for instance, tram route 27 became trolleybus route 627.

Rail travel around the borough changed very little in this period. The major improvement came on the Great Northern Railway side, when in 1906 the company began extending

EARLY MODERNISATION

the line northwards - the eventual terminus would be Stevenage. The first part of the extension took the line to Cuffley, and included in this part of the extension were five new stations: Grange Park just before Enfield, a station to be a replacement for the terminus now called Enfield Chase, Gordon Hill, Crews Hill, and then Cuffley itself. The work included four major schemes over and above the actual extension: these were embankments up to Enfield Chase, an embankment after Enfield Chase up to Gordon Hill, and two big viaducts.

SOUTHGATE c1955 S641039

We are looking towards the tube station.

The Rendlesham viaduct crossed the Maidens Brook valley and Hillyfields, and stands 80 feet high with a total length of 600 feet over 14 spans. It is considered that the viaduct over Sopers Farm is even more spectacular, although not as big. There was a major problem at the beginning when the embankment from Winchmore Hill to Enfield Chase collapsed. This was rebuilt, with the gangers working day and night throughout the very wet December of 1907. The line to Cuffley opened in 1910.

However, no sooner was the extension in operation than the Great Northern Railway Company accepted a tender from McAlpine to take the line onwards. It would be another twelve years before the full extension was completed to Stevenage. Included in this work was a tunnel 2,684 yards long. The work went on through the First World War.

On the Enfield Town service there were no major changes until 1920. The GER introduced a revamped service for Enfield and Chingford known as 'the Jazz Service'. This was an intensive service, which was needed to cover the early mornings and the evening return service. The one service withdrawal occurred thanks to the Southbury Loop. With the introduction of the bus services through to Waltham Cross, the railways found they could not compete. The track remained, and in 1915 the service was started again to assist munitions workers. However, when the First World War ended the service was withdrawn again.

In 1923 rationalisation took place. Up to that time there had been many companies in each region; now in each part of the country all its companies came under one banner. Enfield and its surrounding tracks came under the LNER, the London & North Eastern Railway.

The biggest change in transport in the

ENFIELD A HISTORY & CELEBRATION

SOUTHGATE, AERIAL VIEW c1955 S641022

This view overlooks the tube station. Note the gardens in the bottom of the picture, which are now the site of an office block.

EARLY MODERNISATION

A HISTORY & CELEBRATION

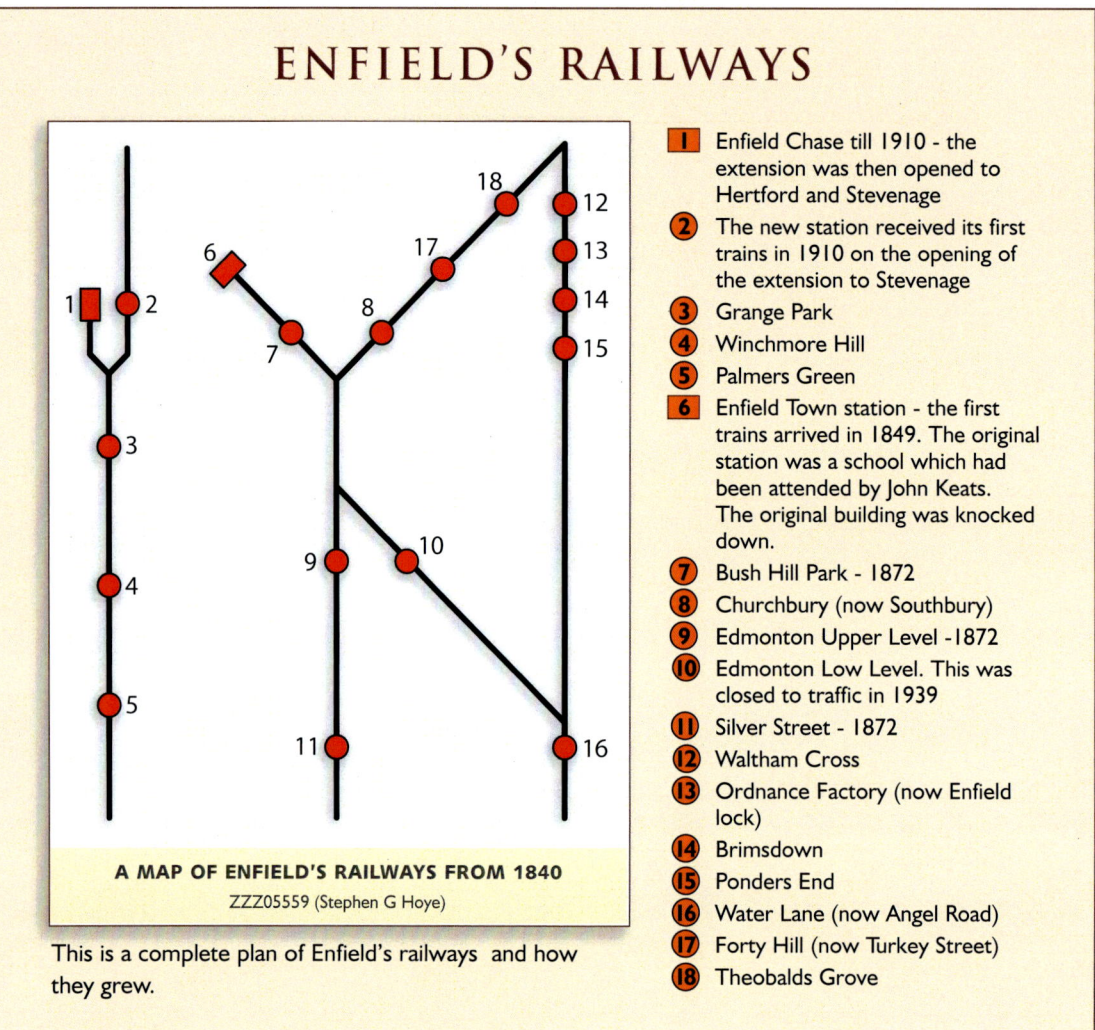

This is a complete plan of Enfield's railways and how they grew.

Fact File

From the mid 1930s onwards, if you had been standing on the platform at Hadley Wood Station you would have seen one or more of the following: Mallard, Sir Nigel Gresley, Union of South Africa, or the Flying Scotsman - all great trains of the steam era.

area was the coming of the Underground. The Piccadilly Line had opened between Finsbury Park and Hammersmith in 1906. The extension to Cockfosters was sanctioned in 1930, and in 1932 the line was opened from Finsbury Park to Arnos Grove. The line was finally completed in 1933 with intermediate stations at Southgate and Enfield West (now Oakwood), and then into Cockfosters.

EARLY MODERNISATION

Cultural pursuits at the beginning of the century consisted either of visiting the local hostelry, where singing and dancing were allowed, or of visiting one of the music halls. As the first years of the century rolled on, hostelries were replaced by public halls as meeting places. It is ironic that most of these public halls were linked to the church. Besides being church halls, a number were also used for lectures and entertainment. There were also others that were turned into music halls. It was at one of these music halls, the Empire, that the great music hall artist Marie Lloyd collapsed. This performance proved to be her last. The Empire music hall had opened in New Road, Lower Edmonton in 1908, but as film started to replace the music hall in the late 1920s and early 30s it was revamped as the Empire Cinema. It was finally knocked down in 1970.

Another well-used hall has been known by two names: St Monica's Church Hall and the Intimate Theatre. It started out as a church hall in 1931 and was revamped in 1937 by John Clements, an actor, into the Intimate Theatre.

With the coming of cinematography (or films, for the uninitiated), shows were given in varying halls around the area. As early as 1909 shows were given in the Grove and the Central Hall in Southgate. Lower Edmonton followed in 1913 and 1916 in the King's Hall. The first large cinema was known as the Alcazar; it opened in Fore Street, Edmonton in 1913. It went through a modernisation program in 1934, only to be severely damaged by a bomb in 1940.

It never recovered its business, and was demolished in 1952.

The following table gives the opening dates of the other halls and cinemas:

1905	St Paul's Parish Hall and Institute
1908	Charles Lamb Memorial Institute, Lower Edmonton
1913	Queen's Hall, Palmers Green Coronation Hall, New Southgate
1914	Halls at Bowes Park, Palmers Green, New Southgate and Bush Hill Park, and in older areas of Edmonton and Southgate
1921	Electric Theatre, Ponders End The Rialto, Enfield Queens Hall, Enfield (rebuilt 1928) Premier, Enfield Highway
1922	Palladium, Palmers Green
1930	The Capitol, Winchmore Hill
1931	St Monica's Church Hall, Palmers Green
1934	The Regal, Edmonton The ABC, Bowes Road
1935	The ABC, Southbury Road
1935	The Odeon, Southgate

Several of the sports clubs in the area had been already established for a number of years at the turn of the century. After the First World War, though, it was a time for them to rebuild and attract new members, as many were lost in the trenches and battles of that war. Cricket, football and most other sports all vied for attention. A public baths had been built in Bradley Road, Enfield Lock in 1893. In 1900 another was added at Knights Lane, Edmonton as part of the Town Hall complex.

Others followed, one at Barrowell Green in 1913, and then Enfield Swimming Pool in 1933. Of these, only Knights Lane still exists. The whole area was revamped in 1970, and is now part of Edmonton Leisure Centre.

Some social improvements had been achieved in the Victorian era, and all the Urban District Councils were to build on these. To begin with, they all initiated a programme of school building. In all, ten new schools were built in the years up to 1914. Of these, nine were for the 5- to 11-year-olds. Schools for pupils aged 12 and upwards were Enfield County, Southgate County and the Convent School. After the First World War another twelve schools were built before the start of the Second World War. This time, nine were primary schools and three were secondary schools.

The subject of education includes literature. Enfield seems to have attracted some of the country's great writers to spend some or all their life in the area, and the following list includes 20th-century writers associated with Enfield:

Thomas Hardy	1840-1928
Jerome K Jerome	1859-1927
Walter Macqueen-Pope	1888-1960
Osbert Sitwell	1892-1969
Stevie Smith	1902-1971
Queenie Leavis	1906-1981
Sir John Betjeman	1906-1984
Paul Scott	1920-1978

The programme of libraries being built only increased by two in Edmonton, at Houndsfield in 1937 and Weir Hall in 1938; two in Southgate, at Bowes Road and De Bohun, both in 1939; and one in Palmers Green in 1940.

The area's hospitals had mostly been built in the late 19th century. However, they had not been originally erected for that purpose - for instance, it was not until 1939 that Chase Farm actually became a hospital; from the turn of the century until that date it had been a home for children. Claverings in Pickets Lock Lane was built in 1902 to cope with the smallpox epidemic. The building was destroyed by fire in 1927, and was not replaced. There was a hospital in Tottenhall Road, Palmers Green, an isolation hospital built in 1902. Grovelands in Southgate became a temporary hospital during the First World War for soldiers wounded on the front. At the end of hostilities it was converted to a convalescent home.

Highlands had been built as an isolation hospital, but in 1939 it was converted to an emergency bed hospital. North Middlesex Hospital was originally the Edmonton Workhouse; it had a separate infirmary block added in 1910, and then in 1915 it became a military hospital dealing with the wounded from the front. In 1920 it returned to civilian use, and was renamed North Middlesex. Further development to it was an outpatients' department in 1922 and a radium department in 1930. St David's had a chequered history. It started life as a Poor Law orphanage, which was closed in 1913. During the First World

EARLY MODERNISATION

WINCHMORE HILL, HIGHLANDS GENERAL HOSPITAL c1960 W482035

The entrance to Highlands Hospital. This is now a housing estate called Highlands Village.

War it was a home for Belgian refugees until 1917, when it became a hospital for epileptics. St Michael's in Chase Side, Enfield had first been an orphanage, and then became a hospital for the elderly and infirm. South Lodge was opened in 1900 as an isolation hospital and remained that way. The War Memorial Hospital was originally called the Enfield Cot Hospital. A new ward was added to the original building in 1906. It was renamed the War Memorial in 1920, and another wing was added in 1926.

St Andrew's Church, built in the 12th or 13th century, stands as majestically today as it has throughout the centuries.

> ## Fact File
> *In the early days of the Second World War, King George VI visited the Royal Small Arms Factory. While on his visit he tested a Bren machine gun which was being made at the factory.*

As for the spiritual needs of the community, many of the Church of England churches had been built before 1900. It is after 1900 that we see more Roman Catholic churches being erected. The list overleaf shows when the more recent churches were built:

73

St Aldhelm's	1903
St John's, Palmers Green	1904-1909
St Edmund's (Roman Catholic)	1905-1907
St Stephen's	1906-1916
St Monica's (Roman Catholic)	1914
St Mary's (Roman Catholic)	1921
Our Lady of Lourdes (Roman Catholic)	1935
Christ the King (Roman Catholic)	1936
St Peter's, Grange Park	1941
St Thomas's	1941

Members of the Jewish faith had been settling in the area for many years. In 1914 a significant number had moved into the Palmers Green area. In 1926, with numbers at a sustainable level, services were taken in various hired halls. A further ten years on, a synagogue was consecrated in Brownlow Road. By 1945 there was a synagogue in the Cockfosters/Oakwood area.

Public services in each of the Urban District Councils were well established, but with an increasing population further work was needed. Before 1900 the water supply was looked after by various water companies or controlled by the UDC: Enfield UDC had a municipal waterworks, while Edmonton and Southgate did not. In 1904 the waterworks were transferred to the Metropolitan Water Board. Just before this, in 1902, a pumping station had been built in Hadley Road. Pumping stations were also built in 1913 at the northern and southern ends of the King George V Reservoir, and there was another in Ramney Marsh in Enfield Lock. A water tower had also been erected in The Ridgeway between 1913 and 1914.

Up to the end of the first decade of the new century, all gas had been supplied from various gas companies. In 1911 all these undertakings were pulled together under the banner of the Tottenham and Edmonton Gas Light and Coke Co. In 1913-14 the Enfield Gas Co was taken over along with its gasworks at Ponders End. The company took over the Waltham and Cheshunt Gas Co (1928), the Hertford Gas Co (1932), the Hoddesdon and Ware Gas Co (1932), the Hitchin Gas Co (1933), the Stevenage Gas Co (1933) and the Southgate Gas Co (1938) - the last-mentioned company had a large gas works at New Southgate. There had been a works in Sydney Road; although the buildings remained, gas had not been manufactured there since 1882. All other works had been transferred to Edmonton by 1921. The exceptions were Cockfosters and Hadley Wood, who were served from Barnet.

An Act of Parliament just before the turn of the century had given the then Enfield Gas Co the right to supply the area with electricity. In 1907 the North Metropolitan Electric Power Supply Co built a power station at Brimsdown, which became commonly known as Northmet Power Station. The area was extended in 1924 after the company acquired land from Trinity College, Cambridge.

The Second World War saw the Enfield

EARLY MODERNISATION

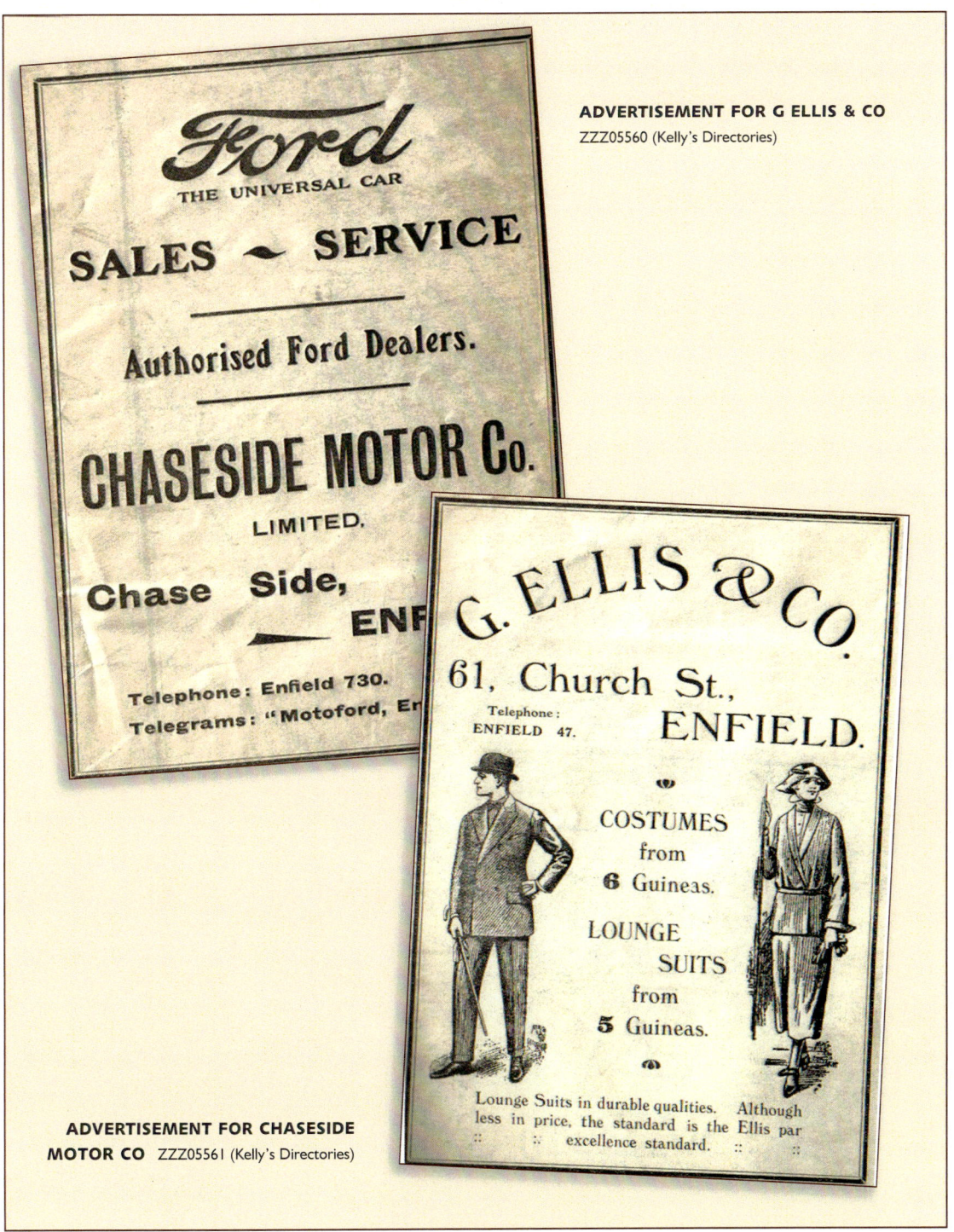

ADVERTISEMENT FOR G ELLIS & CO
ZZZ05560 (Kelly's Directories)

ADVERTISEMENT FOR CHASESIDE MOTOR CO ZZZ05561 (Kelly's Directories)

Here we see advertisements for two local businesses of the time.

ENFIELD A HISTORY & CELEBRATION

THE DEMISE OF THE POWER STATION IN 1976 ZZZ05562 (Enfield Libraries Local History Unit)

This is the demise of the power station. This demolition in 1976 caused a stir and quite a crowd. The author is on the left, the slighter and shorter of the two policemen.

EARLY MODERNISATION

ENFIELD
A HISTORY & CELEBRATION

area finding itself at the mercy of German bombs. Several places were hit, including the Small Arms factory. The photographs here show the damage that the German V1 flying bombs and V2 rockets did; note the Mapleton Avenue photograph especially - the fronts of several houses have been taken off.

THE BRUTALITY OF WAR

These photographs show bomb-damaged areas.

ENFIELD AT WAR, LONDON ROAD c1940
ZZZ05563 (Enfield Libraries Local History Unit)

ENFIELD AT WAR, MAPLETON AVENUE c1940 ZZZ05563 (Enfield Libraries Local History Unit)

EARLY MODERNISATION

"The brutality of the Second World War can be summed up in something my father told me. He had been declared unfit to fight at the front (I believe that he said he was graded 'B2'), so he served in the Home Guard ('Dad's Army'), and worked in various occupations. In 1940 he was working for a builder's firm who had a contract to repair war damage. At the height of the Battle of Britain, he went up on a roof in Ponders End to replace some slates and level up others. What he found when he got up there both shocked him and made him feel very ill. He found a leg in one place, another leg somewhere else, and an arm - he never said if the rest of the body was there or not. He ascertained that these were what was left of a German fighter pilot. Judging from wartime film footage, it appears that the plane must have exploded, causing what my father found."

(Stephen G Hoye)

ENFIELD AT WAR, ABBEY ROAD c1940 ZZZ05563 (Enfield Libraries Local History Unit)

ENFIELD
A HISTORY & CELEBRATION

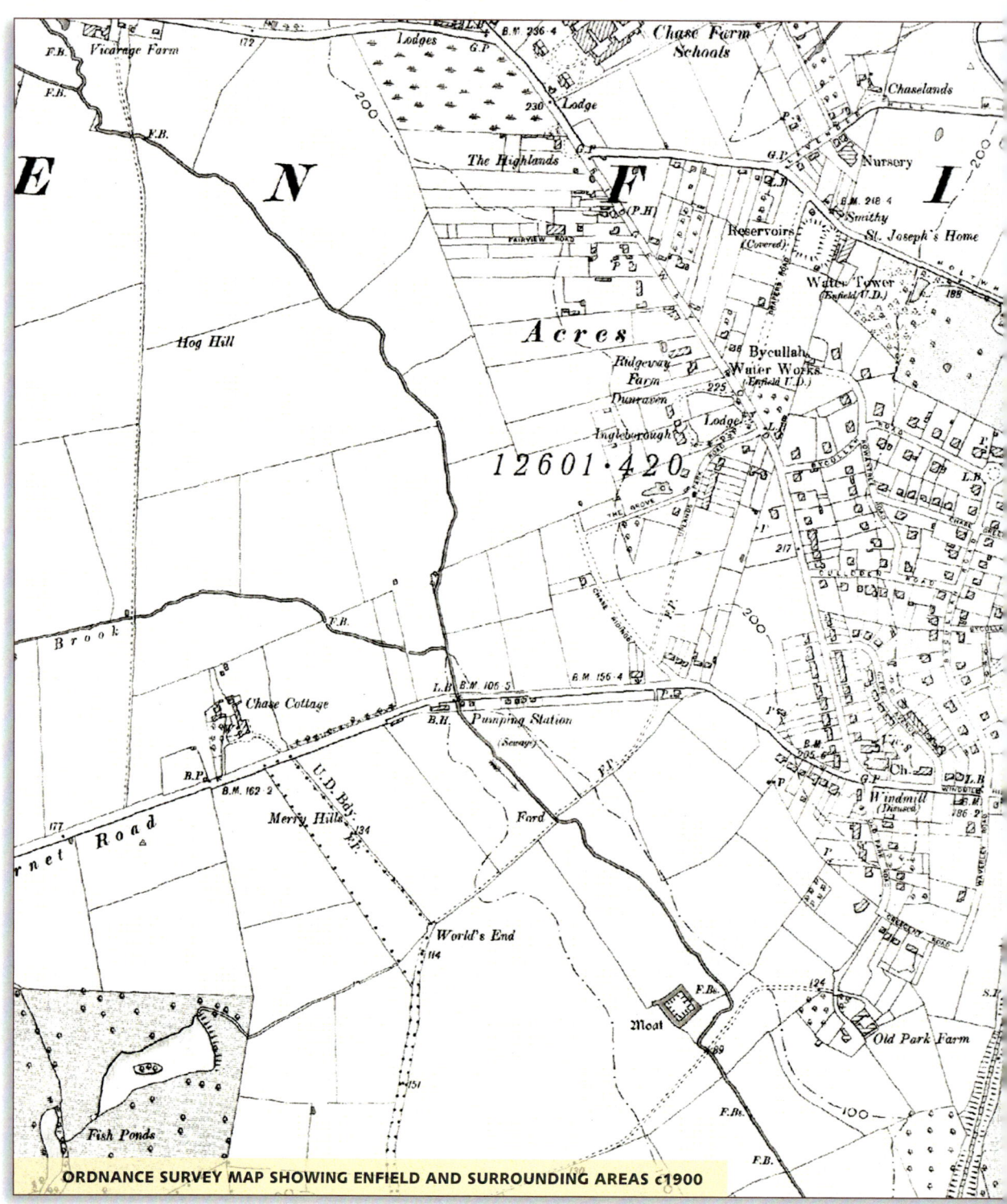

ORDNANCE SURVEY MAP SHOWING ENFIELD AND SURROUNDING AREAS c1900

ORDNANCE SURVEY MAP

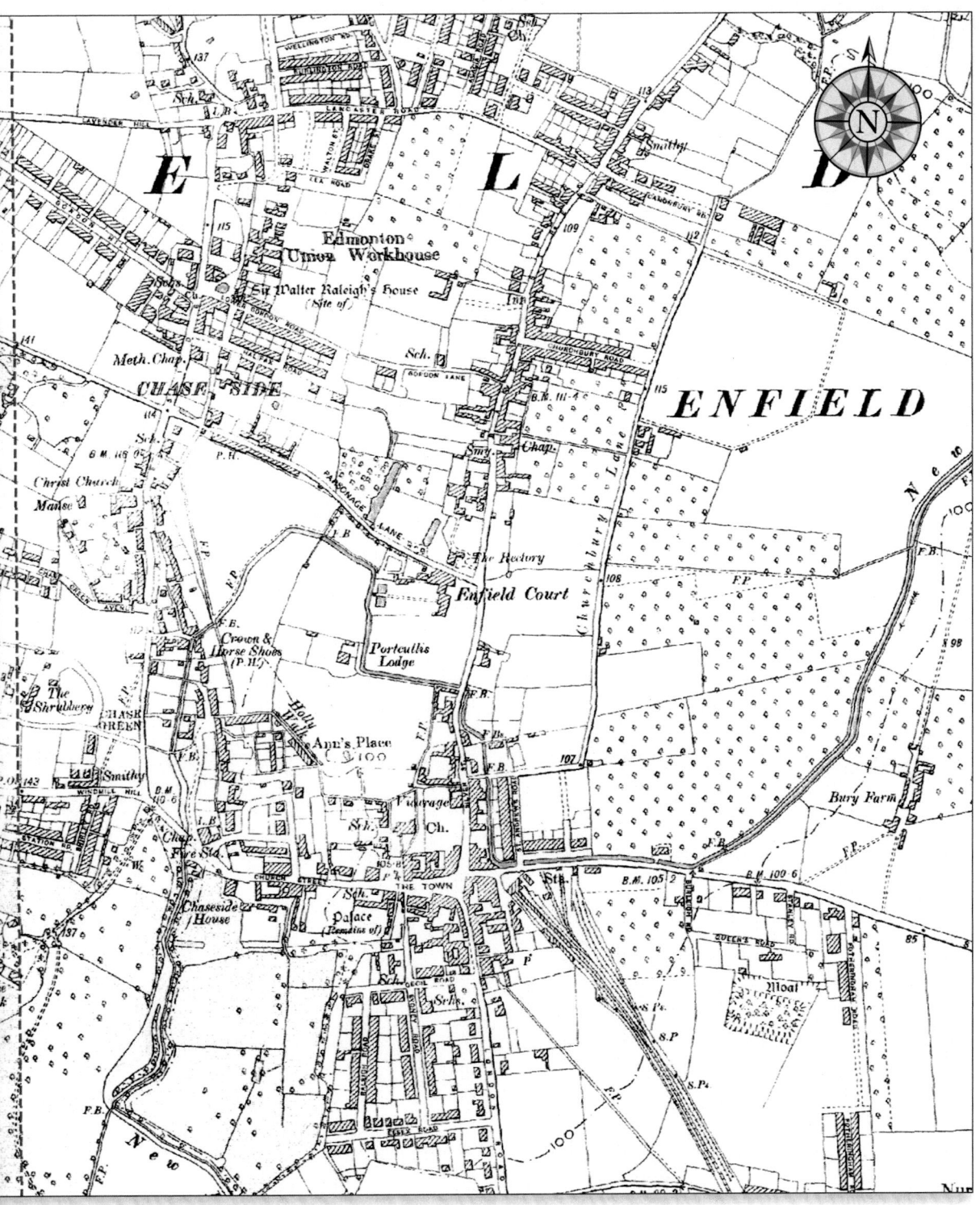

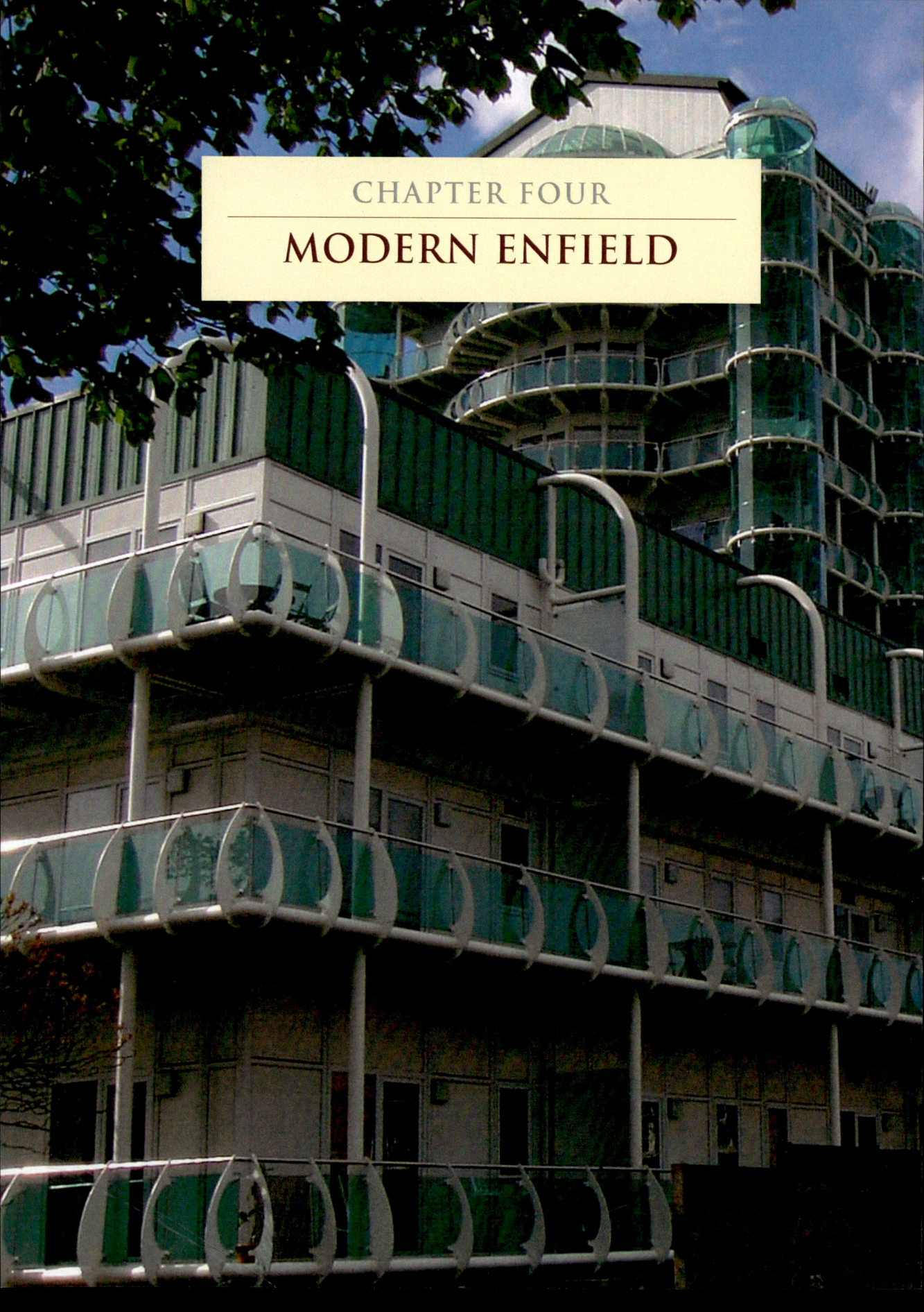

CHAPTER FOUR
MODERN ENFIELD

ENFIELD
A HISTORY & CELEBRATION

PALMERS GREEN, BROOMFIELD HOUSE, BROOMFIELD LANE c1965 P295002

AFTER hostilities had ceased in 1945, there was a lot of patching up to be done - many homes and businesses had been flattened owing to bomb damage. Apart from this post-war infilling, further development has been restricted because of the green belt policy.

Bush Hill Park had one of the largest gaps to be filled. This was in Abbey Road, where a V2 rocket had fallen. The area had started to look as though it had seen betters days; now it was gradually brought back up to scratch. Some of the large houses in Wellington Road and Village Road made way for new cul-de-sacs where either flats or houses were built. Enfield Council compulsory purchased the original cottages in an area off Main Avenue; the council demolished them, and erected flats in their place. Two tower blocks were erected just off the Great Cambridge Road.

There has been very little new building in Cockfosters and Hadley Wood since the end of the war. Where there were gaps these have been filled; but owing to the green belt policy, the area is rural in some parts and urban in others.

Eastern Enfield has seen some major changes. The old cottages in Grove Road and Alma Road, Enfield Wash were knocked down, and both roads disappeared completely. These were replaced by two tower blocks and one road. When the Royal Small Arms Factory closed in 1988, the land was bought by Fairview Estate; this was perhaps the biggest of the redevelopments the borough had seen for some while. Enfield Island Garden Village was built, a total of 1,314 units and a small shopping area. In Bell Lane another two tower blocks were built. To the east of the Great Cambridge Road,

MODERN ENFIELD

the council built a large estate with a small shopping area which is commonly known as the Elsinge Estate; it also included properties on the other side the Great Cambridge Road. On railway land in Carterhatch Lane a further tower block was built.

Green Street changed very little from the point of view of housing. However, one of the houses in Green Street did make the news on a number of occasions. This house had an unwanted visitor, a poltergeist; chairs, tables and beds would move without anyone touching them. It is one of the most intriguing and well-documented cases known, and researchers more or less took over the house with all their equipment. The house has quietened down now, and the researchers have left to ponder their findings.

Both Upper and Lower Edmonton were in a very sorry state. Lack of investment in the area had taken its toll. From the 1950s Edmonton Council, along with private firms built new shops, houses and flats in place of the cottages built in the 1870s for the GER commuters. Edmonton's shopping area had changed little; the market ran from one end of the Green to the other, joining up with Hertford Road. All the market traders stood out in the open. The author can well remember going up and down the market with his parents, especially at Christmas time. Seeing all the poultry hanging there and the various smells wafting in the air made you feel hungry. Customers used to come home well laden, and would sometimes go back there for more the following week.

EDMONTON, BURY LODGE, BURY STREET c1955 E263004

Here people can sit and enjoy the flowers, while the children can enjoy the paddling pool (out of shot).

ENFIELD
A HISTORY & CELEBRATION

CHURCH STREET c1960 E179039

Note a car in the centre of the photograph coming out into Church Street on the left: this where the entrance to the precinct is.

MODERN ENFIELD

ENFIELD
A HISTORY & CELEBRATION

LONDON ROAD c1965 E179042

The number of stationery vehicles shows that traffic has increased, but the lack of vehicles at the junction shows that it is not by much.

In 1965 Edmonton merged with Enfield and Southgate. The new local authority decided to go ahead with Edmonton's plan to redevelop the whole Edmonton Green area. The railway line through Edmonton low-level station was pulled up, and the buildings on the road over the line were demolished. In its place a new covered market and three tower blocks was constructed in 1968. Two other tower blocks were built in Victoria Road - these again replaced some of the cottages that had been there before.

Enfield Town was a town in decline during the post-war years. Many of the shops which had been there for years ceased trading, never to return. They were replaced by building societies, ladies' fashion shops and hair studios. Some parts were redeveloped, and gaps were filled in. The main council development was near Forty Hall, where an area north of Hoe Lane was turned into flats and houses - this was the Worcesters Estate. In London Road, the council pulled down some prefabricated bungalows which had been erected not long after the end of the war. These were replaced by flats, which were completed in 1955 and 1956. For anyone like the author's late parents, who had been renting rooms, these were a godsend. They were one of the first tenants to move into them.

The idea for a ring road around the town was mooted, but this was eventually dropped. There had been many objections

MODERN ENFIELD

to the plan, especially as it was possibly going to interfere with consecrated ground. Enfield Town limped along from decade to decade until 1982. Now at last plans had been laid and permission obtained to build a new shopping precinct, which attracted many new traders to the area like Marks & Spencer, Waitrose and Dixons, as well as existing shops moving to a larger site, like Boots. Since then, the large detached houses have been replaced by blocks of flats, or in the case of Sydney Road, by an eleven-story office block - Tower Point became the home of the former Eastern Gas. However, when the industry was denationalised, work was rationalised, and Tower Point was no longer needed. Eastern Gas moved out, and the building lay dormant for some time. A plan was submitted to Enfield Council, and it was agreed to turn the offices into one- to four-bedroom flats. This work is almost finished, with some of the penthouses being the last to be completed.

Enfield Town seems to be thriving again. It is a strange mix of old and new, with the old being Gentleman's Row, Holly Walk, the Grammar School and St Andrew's Church, and the new being the Shopping Precinct.

TOWER POINT 2005 E179703k (Stephen G Hoye)

A HISTORY & CELEBRATION

> ## Fact File
>
> *Another ghost story concerns Forty Hall. The author has never seen it, but it has been noted and reported that on a moonlight night a lady's hand has been seen rising from the lake. Like all ghost stories, one has to keep an open mind.*

Ponders End, like most of the borough, was in a run-down state after the war. The area had taken a lot of bomb damage, including hits from V1s and V2s. The bomb damage was cleared, and the council took on the redevelopment of the area around Alma Road and South Street. Three tower blocks were built, along with a number of maisonettes. Apart from this, the area remains in a state of

A CORONATION STREET PARTY

In 1953 Queen Elizabeth II was crowned, and many streets held a street party to celebrate the coronation. The street that the author lived in was no exception. Some of the youngest children even went in fancy dress. The two pictures show some of the children who dressed up (the author is on the left, dressed as Sir Gordon Richards, who won the Derby that year, with a friend whose name he cannot remember). The other picture shows the street party itself.

FANCY DRESS 1953 ZZZ05564 (Stephen G Hoye Collection)

MODERN ENFIELD

limbo, neither all old nor all new. Where owners can afford to or want to, the older properties are being modernised and repainted.

After the war Southgate came up against the green belt policy, which prevented further expansion. Apart from replacing the large houses with blocks of flats, very little was done. The shopping areas started to get that tired look; this made shoppers look elsewhere, mainly to Wood Green and Enfield. It is because of the green belt policy that Southgate retains a look about it from the thirties and forties.

Palmers Green has changed hardly at all. Again, as in other parts of the borough after the war, there was some repair work to be done. Some flats have replaced a few large houses, but there has been no further development.

A HISTORY & CELEBRATION

> ### Fact File
>
> *The author was on hand to hear of a ghost story concerning the old Department of Health and Social Security building in High Street, Ponders End. An old lady had been seen walking from north to south through one of the storage rooms before vanishing through a wall. The person who told this had actually seen the ghost.*

New Southgate was also in a very run-down state after the V1 and V2 damage of the war. Southgate Council undertook the redevelopment of the area by building tower blocks in certain parts; this began in 1959 and was completed a year later. They continued with this policy even after the merger into the new London Borough of Enfield in 1965. The work was finally completed during the mid 1970s.

Public transport was in dire straits after the

SOUTHGATE, THE CIRCUS c1960 S641059

MODERN ENFIELD

WINCHMORE HILL, MASON'S CORNER c1960 W482029

Mason's Corner is a well-known local landmark.

war. In some places whole bus fleets were lost through bomb damage, which meant that other areas had to supply any surplus they had. Enfield seemed to manage to maintain a fair service during those difficult years.

The railways, which had been nationalised in 1948, put forward a modernisation plan in 1955; this included the electrification of the services to Enfield Town, Chingford, Hertford and Bishops Stortford. The one omission in this plan was the Lee Valley line - but a surprise inclusion was the Southbury Loop, which had not had any timetabled service since 1912. Work began on it in 1958. It included the re-laying of the track, alterations to the signalling, improvement to bridges, replacing some level crossings, and rebuilding some stations, of which Enfield Town was one. The work took two years to complete, and the new services started in 1960.

The Lee Valley line was eventually electrified in 1969. Here, as before, there were considerable improvements to be made to the line. The track was re-laid, the points changed, the signals upgraded, and the footbridges and road bridges improved; in every case the stations were rebuilt and extended to accommodate the longer trains.

On the roads, the buses gradually returned to normal after the war. Certain older bus types like the STL were replaced, and London Transport brought in the RT to replace them around 1950. No further changes were made until 1960-61, when London Transport withdrew the trolleybuses. They had become like the dinosaurs, creatures of the past: their electrical power source was a remnant of the age of the tram, and they were in need of major expenditure. The routes around the borough retained their numbering to a certain degree, as this table of route number changes shows:

Trolleybus Route No	Bus Route No	Route Run
627	127	Waltham Cross to Tottenham Court Rd
649	149	Ponders End Garage to Liverpool St Station
659	259	Waltham Cross to Holborn Circus
629	269	Enfield Town to Tottenham Court Rd
679	279	Waltham Cross to Smithfield
-	279A	Flamstead End to Smithfield

In this period Enfield saw many other forms of public transport. During the summer months Eastern National ran a service (the X11) from Cecil Road to Southend on Sea. Grey Green and its sister company Orange Luxury coaches ran services to many parts of southern England and East Anglia, as well as to specialist destinations such as Leeds Castle and Stoke Bruerne Canal Boat Museum. Grey Green and Orange Luxury were eventually swallowed by what is now Arriva. When Enfield Town's one-way system came in, the numbers of coaches dwindled.

Industry had been one of Enfield's strong points, and it was sited along the Great Cambridge Road, Lincoln Road, Southbury Road, and the Queensway, in the Brimsdown area, and at the Royal Small Arms Factory at Enfield Lock and the trading estates on the North Circular Road. Many well-known companies had set up their bases in these locations, and even in the hard times after the war they continued to thrive.

The author himself experienced working at one of these firms, the Standard Fuse Company, which was in the Queensway - the company is no longer in existence. At one time three generations of his family including himself worked there. The company was never short of work; in fact, they used to employ homeworkers so as to keep the orders ticking over, and while the author was still in primary school his mother worked from home. The hours were long and the pay was poor even then. What was not known at the time is that the work was also deadly. The author's mother worked using a Bunsen burner on a metal stand; clamped to the stand was a copper bar. At one end of the bar,

MODERN ENFIELD

SOUTHGATE, STATION PARADE c1960 S641056

The rotunda-style buildings of the tube station are now on the listed buildings register.

which was bent, she would put solder, and she would then thread fuses onto wire which was sometimes thinner than human hair. The wire was on a reel, and it was threaded through a needle similar to a sewing needle but a lot longer; then each fuse was in turn soldered at each end by leaving a piece of the wire inside the fuse. She had started this work not long after she left school, and she worked in this environment off and on for about 35 years. It transpires that when the solder was placed on the end of the copper bar, certain impurities were burned off; she breathed in these impurities unknowingly, and this gave her COAD (chronic obstructive airways disease). This is what caused her death in 2002.

Fact File

Alba, who produce radios, TVs, hi-fi systems and personal music systems, used to be based in the borough. Their factory and offices were in Bull Lane, Edmonton, directly opposite North Middlesex Hospital.

ENFIELD
A HISTORY & CELEBRATION

SILVER STREET c1950 E179009

MODERN ENFIELD

A HISTORY & CELEBRATION

> ## ENFIELDS INDUSTRIES
>
> The Standard Fuse Company was just one of Enfield's many industries. Other more well-known companies were Thorn Electrical, which manufactured radios, TVs, lighting, and so on; Reeves, who produced artists' materials; Conway Stuart, who produced pens; and Bellings, noted for cookers and fires. Sangamo Weston, who produced parts for parking meters and control equipment for heating and ventilating systems, were taken over in the late 1970s or early 1980s by Schlumberger, whose extended arm involves oil production. Gor-Ray produced clothing for the fashion trade, and United Flexible Metallic Tubing, more commonly known as UFMT, amongst other things produced flexible parts for central heating systems, hoses for braking and heating for the rail companies, and parts to cover electricity cables. These are just a few of the many companies, some household names, that were or are still operating in the borough.

As the decades went by, Enfield started to lose its industrial image and to take on the role of a commercial centre. Vast swathes of land were cleared all over the borough and made ready for the retail parks which are now in place. It seems ironic that Enfield has gone from being a manufacturing to a retailing base in the space of 20 to 25 years. It is hard to imagine the big industrial complexes standing where Enfield Retail Park and Mandeville Retail Park are now. The picture in Edmonton is much the same; where Tesco, IKEA, Mothercare and several other stores stand, there was once a thriving industrial community.

If the industrial land has not been used for retailing, then it has been used for housing, either council or private. Housing is essential, of course; but when one sees what has happened to the borough's industrial areas, one wonders how many lives have been changed because of the various closures.

After the war several social problems had to be addressed. Where bombs, landmines, doodlebugs and V2s had hit water and sewage pipes, these had to be replaced. Work recommenced on the Girling Reservoir - this was completed by 1951.

As we have seen from the charts earlier in this book, the population had grown quite considerably by this time. This naturally brought an increase in the number of children, and therefore pressure on the schools; this led the various UDCs and subsequently the borough council to carry out extensive improvements. A further 28 schools were built in the period up to 2000.

The borough's library system was expanded, with new libraries opening across the borough. The table on page 99 gives their opening dates and locations. Even with this number of libraries, there are still parts of the borough serviced by the travelling library. For its staff, this can be a lonely and in some areas a challenging job.

As for sport, there have been some big changes. Football and cricket, which have always been the dominant sports, have slowly

MODERN ENFIELD

THE NEW LIBRARIES OF THE BOROUGH OF ENFIELD

Year	Location
1948	Agricola Place (was Fourth Avenue)
1957	Kempe Road (off Turkey Street)
1961	Winchmore Hill (Green Lanes, near the police station)
1962	Ponders End (High Street, opposite the park)
1963	Ridge Avenue (Bush Hill Parade)
1964	Merryhills (Enfield Road)
1966	Southgate High Street
1976	Ordnance Road (Enfield Wash)
1988	Weir Hall (near junction of A406)

been going into decline. The number of minor football leagues has dwindled down to one Saturday and one Sunday league. The heady days through the 1960s, 70s and 80s are long gone. Our senior football clubs, Enfield, Brimsdown Rovers, Cheshunt, Highfield, Cockfosters, and Winchmore Hill have all seen changes in their fortunes.

The biggest shock came with Enfield. Having gone through some torrid times on the pitch, problems arose when their home ground was sold with nowhere prepared for the club to use in future. The club's old home on Southbury Road has changed dramatically. Where the open-air pool and the football ground used to be there now stands a leisure centre, three restaurants and a housing estate. The problems of the club are well documented. Having played at St Albans, Borehamwood, there was a shake-up, and a new club was formed, Enfield Town FC, who play their home games on a ground shared with Brimsdown Rovers. The old Enfield club now share a ground with Ware FC. The ironic thing is that, at the time of writing, the coming season will see both teams in the same league.

The Walker cricket ground at Southgate is used by Middlesex CC for various games, and they have a cricket week every summer there. There are many local cricket clubs, including Enfield, Winchmore Hill, Botany Bay, and Cockfosters, to name but four.

There have been many gains in other recreational societies. There are too many to mention individually, but they range through women's groups, self defence groups, various ethnic societies, and many others, each one having its place in Enfield.

> **Fact File**
>
> *There are over 40 different bus routes which operate within the London Borough of Enfield. These include three all-night routes.*

The hospitals within the borough have met with mixed fortunes. It seemed to be all plain sailing when the 1948 NHS Act was brought in; but this was far from the case. Out of nine hospitals that the borough once had, one is now a geriatric unit, one is under an independent trust, one is now privately run, and just one still comes under the NHS. The other five have been demolished to make way for the inevitable housing. There has been one addition to the nine, but it will only benefit those with private health insurance - it is a Nuffield hospital, which again is privately run.

ENFIELD
A HISTORY & CELEBRATION

THE OPEN-AIR SWIMMING POOL c1955 E179026

MODERN ENFIELD

ENFIELD
A HISTORY & CELEBRATION

HIGHLANDS GENERAL HOSPITAL c1960 W482037

This is now Winchmore General Hospital.

MODERN ENFIELD

ENFIELD
A HISTORY & CELEBRATION

OUR LADY OF MOUNT CARMEL AND ST GEORGE ROMAN CATHOLIC CHURCH 2005 E179704k (Stephen G Hoye)

The new Roman Catholic church is a very interesting building. ITV broadcast one of their morning services from here. There is a family centre at the church where various activities take place, and wedding receptions are held here too.

The Roman Catholic Church of Our Lady of Mount Carmel and St George in London Road, originally built in 1901, suffered major damage in the war - it was virtually demolished by a landmine. The site was cleared, and eventually a new church was built in 1956 in a style that would not look out of place in a new town. St Paul's, New Southgate was repaired, and Ponders End Congregational Church was rebuilt on a new site. Another new church built in 1956-57 was Suffolks Baptist Church.

MODERN ENFIELD

> ## Fact File
>
> *Of the original police stations in Enfield, only one is still in use, albeit on a part-time basis: Winchmore Hill Police Station.*

Enfield as a borough provides quite satisfactorily for its inhabitants, as the author has tried to show in this leisurely stroll from 1945 to the new millennium. However, the Civic Centre is now not big enough for the borough's needs, and plans are being made for it to be extended by also utilising another site.

THE CIVIC CENTRE 2005 E179705k (Stephen G Hoye)

THE CIVIC CENTRE 2005 E179706k (Stephen G Hoye)

CHAPTER FIVE
INTO THE 21ST CENTURY

ENFIELD A HISTORY & CELEBRATION

WHAT of Enfield's future? We have already seen that in the first years of the 21st century, redevelopment is probably going to be the by-word. The former offices of Eastern Gas have already undergone a dramatic change: Tower Point is now 11 floors of one- to four-bedroom flats in the main area and a fitness centre at the south end. Plans have already been submitted for the redevelopment of the north end. As yet planning approval has not been granted, as certain organisations have lodged objections.

SOUTHGATE TECHNICAL COLLEGE c1965 S641062

1 The Duke of Abercorn pub on the right and the old gas offices on the left.
2 The old gas works.
3 The old St Andrew's Primary School building.

The photographs here are reminders of what has been. The author attended St Andrew's School; the site is now occupied by Marks & Spencer.

BUILDING WORK IN ENFIELD ZZZ05573 (Enfield Libraries Local History Unit)

INTO THE 21ST CENTURY

BELOW: The demolition of the Townhouse. This was done this because the front was on London Road. The demolition also saw the demise of the Florida Cinema, which the Townhouse was.

ABOVE: The remains of the Evangelical Church.

LEFT: The Enfield Tavern before demolition. This was in Genotin Road and the demolition was to make way for the new road into London Road, this being part of the revised one way system.

ABOVE: This was the car park on the corner of Cecil Road and Sydney Road. Before this it was where St Andrew's Church Hall and part of St Andrew's Primary School stood along with two houses, the Christian bookshop and the Evangelical Church.

LEFT: This was originally a Lyons Corner House, then Millets, and finally a short term lease shop.

BUILDING WORK IN ENFIELD ZZZ05566 (Ian Bishop-Leggett)

This montage shows some of the building work that Enfield has had to endure lately. The demolition of the Townhouse meant that a building that had been standing since 1911 was no more.

PALACEXCHANGE

Work started in 2004 on the second phase of the precinct. Called PalaceXchange, the work will continue until 2006; this is the first major development in Enfield for nearly 20 years. The pictures show how Phase 2 of the precinct will look, and the map shows the layout of the new precinct. The following information comes from Halogen, who are marketing the precinct: 'The shopping development is being developed by ING Real Estate. Situated alongside Palace Gardens and Church Street, PalaceXchange will link the town centre's three major tenants - Marks & Spencer, Pearson's department store and Woolworth's. The scheme will provide 22 new stores of different sizes, all designed to meet the needs of modern retailers. The scheme also incorporates a new 550-space multi-storey car park and a 40,000 sq ft cultural facility being developed for the London Borough of Enfield, both connected to PalaceXchange via a covered pedestrian bridge. TopShop, New Look, Next, Clarks, Superdrug, TK Maxx and Ottakar's are already committed to the scheme.'

THE NEW PRECINCT AS IT WILL LOOK
ZZZ05568 (Reproduced by courtesy of Halogen, London)

THE NEW PRECINCT AS IT WILL LOOK ZZZ05567 (Reproduced by courtesy of Halogen, London)

INTO THE 21ST CENTURY

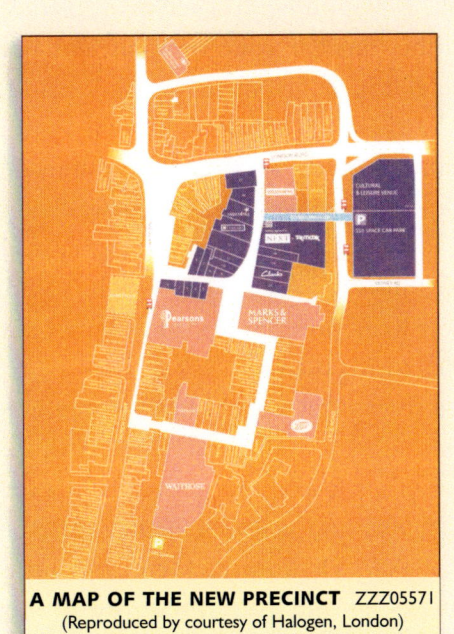

A MAP OF THE NEW PRECINCT ZZZ05571
(Reproduced by courtesy of Halogen, London)

THE NEW PRECINCT AS IT WILL LOOK
ZZZ05570 (Reproduced by courtesy
of Halogen, London)

THE NEW PRECINCT AS IT WILL LOOK
ZZZ05569 (Reproduced by courtesy
of Halogen, London)

Work started in 2004 on the next phase of Enfield's new shopping precinct. However, there is a worrying aspect to Phase 2 of PalaceXchange (see left), and this concerns the turnover of retailers. It is already been seen with Phase 1 that retailers come and go too frequently at times. What causes this? Without specifically asking, one can only surmise that the rent is too high; the number of customers should not be a problem, as the precinct is well used irrespective of the day of the week. Is it the rent that is putting more retailers off from signing up to Phase 2?

One of the biggest improvements is the bus services in the area as a whole - let us hope that it carries on this way. Since de-nationalisation, Enfield, Edmonton, and Southgate have principally become the domain of Arriva, First Bus, and Metroline. The London Borough of Enfield has always been well supplied, but it has been the actual service that has been a let-down. It can be said that the current wages structure for bus drivers is far superior than it has been before, and performance levels have risen quite sharply too; most routes are operating on a schedule of one every ten minutes.

Also, the accommodation on the buses is far better than it used to be, and the buses themselves are more modern. Long gone are the days of a freezing bus with no perceptible heating, and buses that should have been pensioned off years ago. We still get the scenario of two or three coming along together, but with the traffic increasing in the area this still has to be accepted.

ENFIELD
A HISTORY & CELEBRATION

The railways have gone in the other direction since denationalisation. The reliability of the rolling stock is questionable, there are shortages of train crews, and services have been cut back. The Enfield Town to Liverpool Street service used to run every ten minutes at peak times and every twenty minutes off peak. Now it runs every fifteen to twenty minutes at peak times and every thirty minutes off peak - in other words, one train every hour has been cut.

The numbers of cars over the past five years has vastly increased. With the M25 no more than 10 minutes away, every part of the UK is more easily accessible. This is especially good for those who head for the south coast and the ports of Dover and Folkestone; no longer do they need to make lengthy journeys through central London. The building of the M25 has done one good thing for the area: it has reduced the numbers of heavy lorries which are just passing through. However, as with everything else there is an exception to this. The North Circular Road section between near Arnos Grove and Palmers Green is still a bottleneck in both directions. There is at yet no viable solution to make widening the road feasible. A report published just recently by TfL (Transport for London) dated May 2005 is causing friction between the Mayor of London and the community. Further information can be found at www.tfl.gov.uk/streets.

Another major change to Enfield is the reduction of the manufacturing industry. Over the years, the area has seen the demise of the Royal Small Arms Factory, the power station, Thorn Industries, Belling Appliances, plus other smaller concerns that had been in the borough for many years. What has replaced them is commercial activity with a heavy emphasis on the large retail superstore. Enfield Business Park on the southbound carriageway of the A10 is an example. In Edmonton too, each side of the North Circular Road now has big stores rather than manufacturing plants.

This shows that Enfield has become more affluent. Today, a typical three-bedroom house will probably change hands in excess of £200,000, and a leasehold flat in excess of £150,000. Of course, there are always exceptions to the rule; these are average prices. In certain parts of the borough these figures are chicken feed - in these areas house prices are way beyond the average.

Like all parts of London, the ethnic mix here has changed rapidly. When walking around the borough, one can meet residents who come from the four corners of the globe. It is living proof that cultures can mix harmoniously. The changes in the takeaway food shops provides further evidence of the cultural mix: a fish and chip shop now probably serves doner and shish kebabs as well, for instance. The local newsagent will probably be someone who has come from the Indian sub-continent. If we look at our next-door neighbours, we might be surprised at their family background. We have a population that can speak more languages than most people can think of.

Where does Enfield go from here? Quite honestly, it is hard to tell. A lot depends on

INTO THE 21ST CENTURY

CHURCH WALK c1965   E179044

Church Walk is just across from the church. The tall building on the right is Enfield Grammar School; the cottage is attached to the school.

the local council and their attitude. The new part of the precinct is a case in point. The plans had been agreed, but the council seemed to hesitate at the last minute; it was within the final week before work was to commence before they finally agreed to allow the development. The council has admitted, however, that it does not have the funds to fit out a new library within PalaceXchange. They have also announced that some of the space allocated to the Cultural Centre may be given up for further retail use. There is an excellent opportunity for a properly thought-out Cultural Centre to be built within PalaceXchange, but it seems that nobody within the council is interested in any project that may ultimately cost money. It is very short-term thinking: over time, this venue could provide many different uses for the benefit of the community. There is a desperate shortage of good places for outings in Enfield, and it would be a shame if this chance were to slip by. The plan for the library is to develop the existing library in Enfield Town. This will help to keep the west end of the town alive. Exact details of the plans are yet to be released, but let us hope that the council make a good job of it.

Over the past months there has been considerable talk in the local papers of the council selling off various goods and services. It seems that the current Town Hall office space is insufficient for the council's needs, and they are thinking of buying the former Eastern Electricity offices in Carterhatch Lane. This would cost them about £2.5million.

However, a report in the Evening Standard recently stated that Enfield is one of the top ten best places to live in London, and that EN1 was one of the ideal postcodes

ST ANDREW'S PARISH CHURCH c1965 E179043

INTO THE 21ST CENTURY

to settle in. This finding followed a survey by Yellow Pages, which also discovered that EN1 was an area sought-after by couples whose children had left home. One of the reasons for this was the quality of services in the borough. The obvious problem with this kind of report is that it will push house prices up, as the numbers of available houses will diminish. It is a case of one advantage out-weighing the other. Will EN1 still be a good place to live in ten years' time? Let us hope so!

ENFIELD A HISTORY & CELEBRATION

THE OLD COURTHOUSE

THE TOWN 2005

LIBRARY GREEN

CHASE GREEN CENOTAPH

WINDMILL HILL

THE RIVERFRONT

ENFIELD IN 2005 ZZZ05572 (Stephen G Hoye)

This is Enfield today: busy, modern and with a future to look forward to. There are plenty of restful areas as well, as this montage shows.

ACKNOWLEDGEMENTS AND BIBLIOGRAPHY

ACKNOWLEDGEMENTS

The author and publisher gratefully acknowledge the assistance of the following in providing additional illustrative material for use in this book:

Enfield Libraries Local History Unit, Green Lanes, Palmers Green, London N13
Ian Bishop-Leggett
David Pam, Enfield
Halogen, London
Peter Dyer, Photographer, London Road, Enfield
Reed Publishing (Kelly's Directories), Haywards Heath, Sussex

BIBLIOGRAPHY

'A History of Enfield Vol 1: A Parish near London (before 1837)' - David Pam. Enfield Preservation Society 1990
'A History of Enfield Vol 2: A Victorian Suburb (1837 to 1914)' - David Pam. Enfield Preservation Society 1992
'A History of Enfield Vol 3: A Desirable Neighbourhood (1914-1939)' - David Pam. Enfield Preservation Society 1994
'The Royal Small Arms Factory, Enfield, and its Workers' - David Pam. David Pam 1998
Kelly's Directories 1900, 1904, 1923.
'An Illustrated Historical, Statistical and Topographical Account of the Urban District of Enfield' - Cuthbert Wilfrid Whitaker MA. Enfield Preservation Society 1969, reprint of 1911
'British History On Line' - Peter Webster, Editorial Controller. Institute of Historical Research
'Enfield's Past' - Graham Dalling. Historical Publications
London Borough of Enfield Website

Francis Frith
Pioneer Victorian Photographer

Francis Frith, founder of the world-famous photographic archive, was a complex and multi-talented man. A devout Quaker and a highly successful Victorian businessman, he was philosophical by nature and pioneering in outlook. By 1855 he had already established a wholesale grocery business in Liverpool, and sold it for the astonishing sum of £200,000, which is the equivalent today of over £15,000,000. Now in his thirties, and captivated by the new science of photography, Frith set out on a series of pioneering journeys up the Nile and to the Near East.

He was the first photographer to venture beyond the sixth cataract of the Nile. Africa was still the mysterious 'Dark Continent', and Stanley and Livingstone's historic meeting was a decade into the future. The conditions for picture taking confound belief. He laboured for hours in his wicker dark-room in the sweltering heat of the desert, while the volatile chemicals fizzed dangerously in their trays. Back in London he exhibited his photographs and was 'rapturously cheered' by members of the Royal Society. His reputation as a photographer was made overnight.

By the 1870s the railways had threaded their way across the country, and Bank Holidays and half-day Saturdays had been made obligatory by Act of Parliament. All of a sudden the working man and his family were able to enjoy days out, take holidays, and see a little more of the world.

With typical business acumen, Francis Frith foresaw that these new tourists would enjoy having souvenirs to commemorate their days out. For the next thirty years he travelled the country by train and by pony and trap, producing fine photographs of seaside resorts and beauty spots that were keenly bought by millions of Victorians. These prints were painstakingly pasted into family albums and pored over during the dark nights of winter, rekindling precious memories of summer excursions. Frith's studio was soon supplying retail shops all over the country, and by 1890 F Frith & Co had become the greatest specialist photographic publishing company in the world, with over 2,000 sales outlets, and pioneered the picture postcard.

Francis Frith had died in 1898 at his villa in Cannes, his great project still growing. By 1970 the archive he created contained over a third of a million pictures showing 7,000 British towns and villages.

Frith's legacy to us today is of immense significance and value, for the magnificent archive of evocative photographs he created provides a unique record of change in the cities, towns and villages throughout Britain over a century and more. Frith and his fellow studio photographers revisited locations many times down the years to update their views, compiling for us an enthralling and colourful pageant of British life and character.

We are fortunate that Frith was dedicated to recording the minutiae of everyday life. For it is this sheer wealth of visual data, the painstaking chronicle of changes in dress, transport, street layouts, buildings, housing and landscape that captivates us so much today, offering us a powerful link with the past and with the lives of our ancestors.

Computers have now made it possible for Frith's many thousands of images to be accessed almost instantly. The archive offers every one of us an opportunity to examine the places where we and our families have lived and worked down the years. Its images, depicting our shared past, are now bringing pleasure and enlightenment to millions around the world a century and more after his death. For further information visit: www.francisfrith.co.uk

FRITH PRODUCTS & SERVICES

Francis Frith would doubtless be pleased to know that the pioneering publishing venture he started in 1860 still continues today. Over a hundred and forty years later, The Francis Frith Collection continues in the same innovative tradition and is now one of the foremost publishers of vintage photographs in the world. Some of the current activities include:

INTERIOR DECORATION

Today Frith's photographs can be seen framed and as giant wall murals in thousands of pubs, restaurants, hotels, banks, retail stores and other public buildings throughout the country. In every case they enhance the unique local atmosphere of the places they depict and provide reminders of gentler days in an increasingly busy and frenetic world.

PRODUCT PROMOTIONS

Frith products are used by many major companies to promote the sales of their own products or to reinforce their own history and heritage. Frith promotions have been used by Hovis bread, Courage beers, Scots Porage Oats, Colman's mustard, Cadbury's foods, Mellow Birds coffee, Dunhill pipe tobacco, Guinness, and Bulmer's Cider.

GENEALOGY AND FAMILY HISTORY

As the interest in family history and roots grows world-wide, more and more people are turning to Frith's photographs of Great Britain for images of the towns, villages and streets where their ancestors lived; and, of course, photographs of the churches and chapels where their ancestors were christened, married and buried are an essential part of every genealogy tree and family album.

FRITH PRODUCTS

All Frith photographs are available Framed or just as Mounted Prints and unmounted versions. These may be ordered from the address below. Other products available are - Calendars, Jigsaws, Canvas Prints, Mugs, Tea Towels, Tableware and local and prestige books.

THE INTERNET

Over several hundred thousand Frith photographs can be viewed and purchased on the internet through the Frith websites!

For more detailed information on Frith products, look at
www.francisfrith.com

See the complete list of Frith Books at: www.francisfrith.com
This web site is regularly updated with the latest list of publications from The Francis Frith Collection. If you wish to buy books relating to another part of the country that your local bookshop does not stock, you may purchase on-line.

For further information, trade, or author enquiries please contact us at the address below:
The Francis Frith Collection, Unit 19 Kingsmead Business Park, Gillingham, Dorset SP8 5FB.
Tel: +44 (0)1722 716 376   Email: sales@francisfrith.co.uk

See Frith products on the internet at www.francisfrith.com

FREE PRINT OF YOUR CHOICE
CHOOSE A PHOTOGRAPH FROM THIS BOOK
+ POSTAGE

Mounted Print
Overall size 14 x 11 inches (355 x 280mm)

TO RECEIVE YOUR FREE PRINT

Choose any Frith photograph in this book

Simply complete the Voucher opposite and return it with your payment (to cover postage and handling) and we will print the photograph of your choice in SEPIA (size 11 x 8 inches) and supply it in a cream mount ready to frame (overall size 14 x 11 inches).

Order additional Mounted Prints at HALF PRICE - £19.00 each (normally £38.00)

If you would like to order more Frith prints from this book, possibly as gifts for friends and family, you can buy them at half price (with no additional postage costs).

Have your Mounted Prints framed

For an extra £20.00 per print you can have your mounted print(s) framed in an elegant polished wood and gilt moulding, overall size 16 x 13 inches (no additional postage required).

IMPORTANT!

❶ Please note: aerial photographs and photographs with a reference number starting with a "Z" are not Frith photographs and cannot be supplied under this offer.

❷ Offer valid for delivery to one UK address only.

❸ These special prices are only available if you use this form to order. You must use the ORIGINAL VOUCHER on this page (no copies permitted). We can only despatch to one UK address.

❹ This offer cannot be combined with any other offer.

As a customer your name & address will be stored by Frith but not sold or rented to third parties. Your data will be used for the purpose of this promotion only.

Send completed Voucher form to:
**The Francis Frith Collection,
1 Chilmark Estate House, Chilmark,
Salisbury, Wiltshire SP3 5DU**

Voucher for **FREE** and Reduced Price Frith Prints

Please do not photocopy this voucher. Only the original is valid, so please fill it in, cut it out and return it to us with your order.

Picture ref no	Page no	Qty	Mounted @ £19.00	Framed + £20.00	Total Cost £
		1	Free of charge*	£	£
			£19.00	£	£
			£19.00	£	£
			£19.00	£	£
			£19.00	£	£
			£19.00	£	£

*Please allow 28 days for delivery.
Offer available to one UK address only*

* Post & handling	£3.80
Total Order Cost	£

Title of this book ....

I enclose a cheque/postal order for £ ....
made payable to 'Heritage Resource Management Ltd'

OR please debit my Mastercard / Visa / Maestro card, details below

Card Number:

Issue No (Maestro only):   Valid from (Maestro):

Card Security Number: Expires:

Signature:

Name Mr/Mrs/Ms ....
Address ....
....
....
.... Postcode ....
Daytime Tel No ....
Email ....

Valid to 31/12/26

Free Print – see overleaf

Can you help us with information about any of the Frith photographs in this book?

We are gradually compiling an historical record for each of the photographs in the Frith archive. It is always fascinating to find out the names of the people shown in the pictures, as well as insights into the shops, buildings and other features depicted.

If you recognize anyone in the photographs in this book, or if you have information not already included in the author's caption, do let us know. We would love to hear from you, and will try to publish it in future books or articles.

An Invitation from The Francis Frith Collection to Share Your Memories

The 'Share Your Memories' feature of our website allows members of the public to add personal memories relating to the places featured in our photographs, or comment on others already added. Seeing a place from your past can rekindle forgotten or long held memories. Why not visit the website, find photographs of places you know well and add YOUR story for others to read and enjoy? We would love to hear from you!

www.francisfrith.com/memories

Our production team

Frith books are produced by a small dedicated team at offices near Salisbury. Most have worked with the Frith Collection for many years. All have in common one quality: they have a passion for the Frith Collection.

Frith Books and Gifts

We have a wide range of books and gifts available on our website utilising our photographic archive, many of which can be individually personalised.

www.francisfrith.com